Joss Whedon

THE GENIUS BEHIND *BUFFY*

Candace Havens

TITAN BOOKS

JOSS WHEDON: THE GENIUS BEHIND BUFFY

1 84023 727 9

Published by
Titan Books
A division of
Titan Publishing Group Ltd
144 Southwark St
London
SE1 0UP

First Titan edition August 2003
1 3 5 7 9 10 8 6 4 2

Published by arrangement with BenBella Books, PO Box 601389,
Dallas, TX 75360, USA.

Joss Whedon: The Genius Behind Buffy copyright © 2003
by Candace Havens. All rights reserved.

Design and supplemental materials © 2003 Ben Bella Books.

Interior design and composition by John Reinhardt Book Design.

Did you enjoy this book? We love to hear from our readers.
Please e-mail us at: readerfeedback@titanemail.com or write to
Reader Feedback at the above address.

To subscribe to our regular newsletter for up-to-the-minute news, great offers
and competitions, email: titan-news@titanemail.com

Titan books are available from all good bookshops or direct from our mail
order service. For a free catalogue or to order, phone 01536 76 46 46 with
your credit card details or contact Titan Books Mail Order, Unit 6, Pipewell
Industrial Estate, Desborough, Kettering, Northants NN14 2SW, quoting
reference JW/GB.

A CIP catalogue record for this title is available from the British Library.

Printed and bound in Great Britain by MPG, Bodmin, Cornwall.

To the people, Steve, Don, Peg and Helen,
who believe in me no matter what.

And to Glenn,
who is the master of making dreams come true.

Contents

Introduction

"I wanted *Buffy* to be a cultural
phenomenon, period . . . that was always the plan."

—Joss Whedon

In his scruffy jeans and baggy button-down camp shirt, Joss Whedon doesn't look much like a Hollywood mogul. Joss is soft-spoken and funny. His lopsided grin makes you think more of the video-store clerk he once was than the man who created one of the most beloved television shows of all time.

From its inauspicious beginnings as a midseason replacement on the fledgling WB network, *Buffy the Vampire Slayer* has become a phenomenon. *Rolling Stone* called it "the coolest show on TV." *Entertainment Weekly* proclaimed it "the best drama on television." *Buffy* was ranked the number-one show in America by the *Pittsburgh Post Gazette*, number five by *TV Guide,* and one of the top ten by *USA Today*.

In 2000, Joss garnered an Emmy nomination for the episode of *Buffy* titled "Hush," and, in the same year, the series was honored with the Founder's Award from Viewers for Quality Television. Joss has been nominated for countless awards (he recently won a Best Genre Network Series Saturn Award for *Buffy*) and has been listed as one of *Entertainment Weekly's* top ten people in Hollywood.

But, most important, in *Buffy,* Joss created a new icon. And it didn't happen by accident. "I always intended for *Buffy* to be a cultural phenomenon," Whedon confesses. "That's how I wrote it. In the back of your mind, you're picking up your Oscar and your Saturn and everyone is playing with their *Buffy* dolls."

Joss wins the Saturn!

ALBERT L. ORTEGA

Joss Whedon has become one of Hollywood's hottest properties. He recently found himself producing three television series on three different networks (*Buffy* on UPN, *Angel* on WB, and *Firefly* on Fox) with two more, *Buffy the Animated Series* and *Ripper*, in the planning stages. He wrote the popular *Fray* comic-book series, was nominated for an Oscar for the *Toy Story* screenplay, and has written or contributed to numerous films, including *Speed*, *Alien Resurrection*, and *X-Men*.

Even in the rarified world of Hollywood producers, Joss stands out as an unusual individual. A brilliant writer, he is equally adept at drama, comedy, horror, and action. A producer with a self-proclaimed feminist agenda, Joss makes a point of defying convention and Hollywood norms.

A shy, reclusive child, Joss has overcome his inherent introversion to achieve great success in a variety of leadership roles: as a head writer, producer, and director. Genuinely kind and easygoing, Joss is also a perfectionist and "control freak" who oversees most every aspect of his productions. And, when necessary, Joss can be ferocious in protecting his creations.

So, who is Joss Whedon? What makes him tick? And, most important, how does he manage to create such magic?

Growing Up

"Most people really don't get along that well with their own families."

—Joss Whedon

As any fan of *Buffy* knows, Joss loves anguish. Each season the characters suffer from traumas of every kind, from impossible love to hopeless addiction. The majority of Whedon's characters come from unhappy or broken homes. Buffy's father left, not even returning at her mother's death. Angel's father was demeaning and cruel. Xander's household was a drunken brawl while Willow's mother was cool and aloof.

So what was Joss's childhood like? Was it terribly traumatic? Was he beaten and tortured? Did his parents lock him in his room where his lonely mind began to generate the fantasies that would some day make him famous?

Joss, who grew up in Manhattan, swears he had a normal and quite boring childhood. Joss was born Joe Whedon on June 23, 1964, the youngest of three boys (he would later have two younger step-siblings). Joss was born into a television dynasty. His grandfather, John Whedon, was a writer on *The Andy Griffith Show*, *The Dick Van Dyke Show*, *The Donna Reed Show*, *Room 222*, and *Kilroy*.

His father, Tom Whedon, was an Emmy-winning television producer and writer who worked with the shows *Golden Girls*, *Alice*, *Electric Company*, *Captain Kangaroo*, *The Dick Cavett Show*, and *Benson*. Earlier in his career, Tom Whedon wrote musicals, later one of Joss's passions.

Joss's mother, Lee Stearns, was a high-school teacher, aspiring novelist, and, in Joss's words, "whupass personified." "She was very smart, uncompromising, cool as hell," Joss relates. "You had to prove yourself—not that she wouldn't come through if you didn't, but she expected you to hold your own."

"My mom is a very bright woman, who believed in education," said Joss. "You don't always appreciate that when you are a kid, but I do now." Joss's mother was much like the female characters Whedon likes to create. Like Tom Whedon, she also had her musical side, acting and singing in summer-stock productions. Whedon's musical talents clearly came from both sides of the family.

Joss's parents divorced when he was nine. He lived with his mother and spent his summers in New York with his mother and stepfather at a sort of informal "artists' commune."

Joss was a shy, imaginative, and easily frightened child. "I was afraid of the dark and everything, and I had a vivid imagination. People think I'm joking when I say that I was a strange, unlovable child. But it is true. I think the thing that I was most afraid of was my big brother. If you see big brothers being eviscerated on the show you'll know where that came from."

> People think I'm joking when I say that I was a strange, unlovable child. But it is true.
> —Joss

As a child Joss spent many hours alone making up stories and games with his toys. Each toy had certain role to play in Joss's imagination and every day was a new story. When he was eleven or twelve, for example, he invented a story featuring hero Harry Egg, itinerant space traveler, and his androgynous demigod sidekick, Mouseflesh. Whedon discovered early on that he could escape from the rest of the world by slipping into one of his imaginary stories.

"I was the sad, unlovable child, who had a perfectly normal childhood," says Whedon of his early years. "I never felt like anything was right in life and I didn't understand why it seemed so easy for everyone else. There are people who feel a little odd all of their lives; I think I was destined to be one of those people," Whedon laughs.

Whedon doesn't like to talk about his family. He wants to respect their privacy as much as possible, but he does say he comes from loving parents. "I'm not sure my parents ever understood me, and I'm certain they thought I was a little strange. But they loved me. No, they didn't lock me in closets or beat me. I was just born this way."

If he wasn't making up imaginary games with his toys he was reading books, in particular comic books and science fiction. Hours were spent in his room as Joss read and reread the new issues of *Dracula, Spider-Man,* and *Fantastic Four.* It wasn't long before he was reading every science-fiction book he could get his hands on. Frederick Pohl and Frank Herbert were among his favorite authors.

"In a lot of ways those worlds made a lot more sense to me than the one I lived in," Joss says. "Every opportunity I had to lose myself in those stories I took and I'm sure they influenced me in some ways even I don't know."

Joss was pretty much a loner and he spent much his time in front of the television. Watching television became another form of escape and one he admits he used "way too often." But all those hours in front of the TV ultimately paid off.

"As a very young child I watched a lot of cartoons, but not really things in prime time. As I grew older I didn't watch a lot of American television . . . I was beyond that. I watched *Masterpiece Theatre* and *Monty Python.* It's sad, I know, but I wanted to be British. I had this fascination with England that's almost absurd when I look back on it now."

His fascination with film also began at an early age. Some of his earliest memories were of watching films, and he has studied them his whole life. Early on he had a penchant for scary movies—"the cheesier the better," he says. "Even a bad horror film can scare you, and my mind was so gullible when I was a kid. I could make everything seem so real to myself." To this day he still enjoys horror films, good or bad.

His mind never stopped going into overdrive. From an early age he would tell his mother the strange stories he made up and, while she encouraged his creativity, "I'm sure more than once there were times when she questioned my sanity. I would have," laughs Whedon.

As he grew older, his imaginary worlds became filled with crazy characters who lived in ultracool universes and had all kinds of special powers. There were times when he would create such frightening stories that he would actually scare himself.

At some point the shy young Joss discovered something magical. When he was about eleven years old, he realized he could make people laugh. During an interview, he was asked where his sense of humor came from. "There were times when I didn't feel as though I was getting attention I deserved, and I learned that if you said something funny, people would stop and listen," says Whedon. "At least for a little while."

Joss the Feminist

"I was an androgynous little thing. I had masses of curly red hair and old ladies would always come up and say, 'Oh, I love her hair.'"

—Joss Whedon

Whedon is a writer with a self-declared "feminist agenda," and *Buffy* was designed from the onset as an unabashedly feminist show. While one can quibble with the feminist credentials of a show featuring so many attractive women in sexy outfits, Joss takes *Buffy*'s feminist credentials very seriously. He considers Buffy one of a handful of genuinely tough female characters that ever made it to the screen.

"There was that thing in the '80s where every woman in a film had to have a pointless karate scene—for no reason," Joss complains. "Like *Wayne's World*! They had to do karate to show they were tough and then go back to being meaningless in the narrative. Or helpless. People were attempting something good, but the only person who was putting actual tough women out there was [James] Cameron. He was just kicking ass. He gave us the two great prototypes—Ripley and Sarah Connor.

> James Cameron gave us the two great prototypes—Ripley and Sarah Connor. —Joss

"I've always felt comfortable with women as people," Joss adds, "and I was surprised when I realized how few people—writers and filmmakers—actually think of them as people."

Joss's feminism seems to have started early. A lonely child, intimidated by his father and older brothers, Joss formed a close attachment to his mother. "It starts with my mother. It always starts with my mother. She was an extraordinarily strong, independent, tough, uncompromising, cool, funny person. She taught me most of what I know about everything."

Joss credits two other strong women with influencing his life. One is Jeanine Basinger, his film professor from Wesleyan, who remains a close friend to the present day. "My professor Jeanine Basinger is an extraordinary person. She is extremely simple in her ethics and her

Director James Cameron and Linda Hamilton, who plays the eerily tough Sarah Connor in the *Terminator* series.

Joss and his wife Kai Cole.

presentation and in her loyalties, but her lectures are so dense I can't follow them. She is truly brilliant. A lot of people who have met both her and my mother remarked on the similarities."

The other is Joss's wife, Kai Cole, whom he credits with having a significant effect on him. "When you asked about the women who influenced me, she would be the third. My wife is enormously strong . . . [she] is a complete self-starter. She is a constant inspiration to me."

> those women just attract me. It's embarrassing, almost. —Joss

It's clear that Joss finds strong women both inspiring and, well, sexy. "Oh, you know—I like strong women. I was raised by one. I don't see many of them and I see a lot of bullshit pretending . . . also, those women just attract me. It's embarrassing, almost. A lot of it is inherent and studied and strongly felt feminism, and a lot of it is just that chicks are cool."

While happy to portray tough, sexy women on *Buffy*, Whedon is careful not to go over the line into exploitation. As a fan of comics, and creator of one of his own, he's clearly embarrassed by the increasingly sexual trend of *manga* (Japanese comics). "I'm a big fan of puberty and people who've been through it," he insists.

Whedon goes on to say: "There's a comics artist I won't name who I've talked to. His creation is really popular, I guess, but there's this weird thing, where I guess she was molested, and that's part of the story. But you know, she's a young girl who looks like a *Playboy* model in her undies. I wanted to molest her, too, you know? The message that sends is weird, and I don't go for it.

"Because of stuff like that I went away from comics for a long time. Everything seemed to be soft-core and all of it was disguised as empowerment. 'I have the power to have my shirt ripped, and now you can see my nipples! Ah-ha!'"

Whatever Joss's feminist credentials, there is no escaping his insights into the female psyche. "Ask him who the role models are," says Professor Basinger. "Joss has a wonderful, strong mother. He appreciates women who are strong. His wife is a strong woman and I like her enormously. He knows women better than even he would ever admit."

> I have the power to have my shirt ripped, and now you can see my nipples! Ah-ha! —Joss

"He definitely has that ability to get in their heads," agrees David Greenwalt (former executive producer of *Angel*), "better than anyone I've ever known. I'd say I'm in touch with my feminine side to a certain degree, but nothing like Joss."

"I know this is going to sound weird, but I always wondered if maybe there was a little bit of Willow in Joss," laughs Alyson Hannigan (Willow). "I don't mean he's girly or anything. He's definitely a manly man. But there's this sensitivity to him where women are concerned. He gets girls. He understands how we think. He's also incredibly easy to talk to and fun at the same time. I've always wondered how he knew so much about women, without actually being one. He gets in our head way too easy.

> I always wondered if maybe there was a little bit of Willow in Joss. —Alyson Hannigan

"Oh, great, I know that quote is going to get me in trouble, somehow, someway. But you know what I mean. He just gets us."

Joss often made home movies, enrolling his family as the cast. He would make sure that everyone understood what they were supposed to do and he created cute little films that still make his family laugh today.

That sense of humor came in handy when Joss faced the greatest trial of his young life—high school! Joss was sent to an exclusive private high school, the Riverdale High School in Upstate New York. It was the worst time of his life. "[At Riverdale] I learned more about rejection than I ever cared to," says Whedon.

> There were times when I didn't feel as though I was getting attention I deserved, and I learned that if you said something funny, people would stop and listen.
> —Joss

When his mother went on sabbatical to England, Joss jumped at the chance to go with her. "[My mother] was a teacher and she didn't believe there were schools in Los Angeles where my father lived. She didn't believe such a thing could exist. She was a terrible snob. By some weird happenstance I got into the best [high] school in the country [Winchester College]. I really shouldn't have and I can't stress that enough. It was a fluke. And so I went over for half a year and when my family went back, I stayed."

A longtime Anglophile, Joss was thrilled at the prospect of living in England and studying at a famous British institution. Boasting the longest unbroken history of any school in England, Winchester College was founded by Bishop William of Wykeham in 1382. Winchester has an ancient, medieval feel about it, and at first Joss was truly delighted to be there.

> [At Riverdale] I learned more about rejection than I ever cared to. —Joss

"I was always wanting something that I couldn't have when it came to relationships in high school. Then I had the chance to go to Winchester, which is a boarding school in England. . . . The rejection wasn't so bad there because it was all boys," Whedon laughs. "I jumped at the chance because of course the idea of being British was extremely appealing."

Despite Joss's initial enthusiasm, he soon found that alienation and loneliness followed him to Winchester. While he loved all things British, he soon discovered that the Brits were not equally fond of Americans, and it was difficult to fit in. It was a rude awakening when Whedon, who had spent many years watching British television series, discovered that people in England weren't quite like the actors he had seen in the *Monty Python* skits.

the idea of being British was extremely appealing. —Joss

Joss spent a good deal of his time sneaking away from school on the weekends to go into town and watch whatever films might be available. It was his chance to once again lose himself in his own magical world.

And he desperately needed the escape. In the boarding houses where Whedon lived, thirteen boys, called Commoners, shared a single room. The house was ruled by a housemaster and discipline was strongly emphasized. He found relationships with his instructors difficult, although there were a few that he appreciated. "Like anywhere, you have good and bad instructors," Joss says. "The idea for Mr. Giles came from Winchester, so it wasn't all bad."

"You know, I don't think my experience in high school was any worse than anyone else's, to be honest," Whedon admits. "I just know that it was a horrible experience for me. Girls didn't know I existed, and quite honestly even if they did I wouldn't have known what to do with them. I tried once to get a girl to notice me in high school, but it didn't work. Of course it never helped that I went to an all-boys school. I don't think you learn the things you need to know about the opposite sex, when you spend so much time with your own."

I tried once to get a girl to notice me in high school, but it didn't work. —Joss

A keen observer, Joss studied his classmates. He could understand what made some kids popular and others not, but he couldn't make the formula work for himself. Like many high school students, Joss had a difficult time adjusting. He was in a new country, with people he hardly knew. The boarding school was nothing like his home in Manhattan, and his family, his mother in particular, was thousands of miles away.

Joss's difficult high school experiences powered the angst and power of *Buffy*, particularly in its beginning years. Many of the early plots came directly from his high school experiences. Whedon, for example, tells of drawing a self-portrait in high school with his hand disappearing. He felt that he was invisible, unimportant, and unappreciated. In "Out of Sight, Out of Mind," a first-season *Buffy* episode, Whedon developed a story about a high school girl who was so ignored she literally disappeared.

> The very funny, realistic guy I knew shuffling around in sneakers here at Wesleyan is the exact same guy you meet when you step into his office at Mutant Enemy.
> —Jeanine Basinger

"I was nowhere close to being a popular kid in high school, I just sort of went and hoped for the best every day. There were days when I wondered if anyone else in the world knew I existed. You'll see that plot a lot in the early days of *Buffy*, because that sense of isolation is in almost all of us. Really, there are few people who get away from high school without going through some kind of trauma. Most of us dealt with it on a daily basis. I wish my high school years could have been different. I wish that I was Mr. Popular, but then I would be writing very different shows."

After graduating from Winchester, Joss Whedon attended the elite Wesleyan University in Wesleyan, Connecticut. College was a different experience from high school, and Whedon soon learned he could be more creative and that his opinion was valued. While far from the big man on campus, Joss made friends and began to have a life. He played Dungeons and Dragons and threw himself into his film studies. "College rocked," Whedon tells. "I was miserable most of the time, but in a party way." Joss had found an environment where his imagination could flourish. And, most important, he could be himself and feel accepted.

> I wish that I was Mr. Popular, but then I would be writing very different shows. —Joss

Most of his instructors remember him fondly, not because he is famous now, but because even in those early days he was the self-effacing, creative guy he is today. Whedon's former professor Basinger says, "The very funny, realistic guy I knew shuffling around in sneakers here at Wesleyan is the exact same guy you meet when you step into his office at Mutant Enemy." Basinger is the chair of the film studies program and the Corwin-Fuller professor of film studies and American studies at Wesleyan. "Joss was one of the all-time best film majors I ever had," Basinger continues. "He was born with the narrative instincts and the intelligence that makes him who he is. We gave him a place to grow." To this day she regularly chats with Whedon on the phone.

The respect was mutual. "I walked out with unbelievably essential knowledge," says Whedon. "I happened to study under the people that I believe are the best film teachers ever. Film hasn't existed that long, so I say that with a certain amount of confidence. The teachers at Wesleyan were brilliant, the most brilliant people I've been around, and there is not a story that I tell that does not reflect something I . . . [learned]. . . from my professors. They left me with some incredible insights into film, and the encouragement to think I might be able to make something of myself."

Joss with his favorite professor, Dr. Jeanine Basinger.

BILL BURKHART

Interview with Jeanine Basinger,
Corwin-Fuller professor of film
studies and American studies
at Wesleyan University

HAVENS: *What kind of student was Joss?*

PROFESSOR BASINGER: Joss was a superior student. I teach at a very elite university and in a program that draws the top students. But he was the top of the top, the crème de le crème. There are four or five people I've had that were just beyond belief, and he was one of them.

I don't know if you are familiar with our university or all of the alumni we have who are enormously successful in the film business. People like David Kohan who did *Will and Grace*. Jennifer Crittenden (*Everybody Loves Raymond*) who wrote for *Seinfeld* and the *Drew Carey Show*. Jeffery Lane (*Bette*) who did *Mad About You*. There was Michael Bay (director, *Pearl Harbor, Armageddon, The Rock*), Miguel Arteta (director, *The Good Girl, Six Feet Under, Chuck & Buck*) and Akiva Goldsman (writer, *A Beautiful Mind, Practical Magic, The Recruit*).

Out of all of this Joss still stood out. He's incredibly smart. He is deeply, widely read. He's not one of those people who falls into show business because he taps the popular culture and nothing else. He has read the classics. He knows history. His mother was a great schoolteacher. He was raised by a wonderful teacher, and he reflects that. He is a joyous student. He loves to learn. All of that stuff that you see in *Buffy*, all that greatness, is a product of someone who has had a superior liberal arts education, coupled with a superior mind and imagination.

HAVENS: *Could you see the creativity and potential when he was a student?*

PROFESSOR BASINGER: I saw it in the first papers he wrote for me. He always pushed. He's a really good film historian. He continues to grow and learn. He likes to come East and I set up private screenings for he and I and his wife Kai at the Museum of Modern Art. I pick out rare things. Silent films, *Woman of the World*, or a good color print of *Some Came Running* or *Bonjour Tristesse*. He continues to study and grow and learn. I think that's something that does set genius apart. Most people have an idea that a genius is someone who never studies, or works hard. It's quite the opposite.

HAVENS: *He says he's always wanted to make films. What were his student films like?*

PROFESSOR BASINGER: His senior student film, which he would be happy if I didn't mention, is a *Buffy* prototype. It's a girl whose prom date turns out to be a vampire. But he doesn't want [you] to hear about this. In our program students study film . . . history and theory. They know how to break a film down and see how it works and they work hands on and make films. On the other hand, it's an undergraduate program and liberal arts school. We are not a filmmaking factory. [Students] take literature, learn a language, play an instrument. He did all that and it prepared him for the thinking process more than the technical filmmaking process. Even though he had written, produced, directed, and edited his own film, it isn't the same as doing an undergraduate film program at USC or NYU or something like that.

HAVENS: *Do you know who some of his early influences were in the film world?*

PROFESSOR BASINGER: He loves the work of Otto Preminger (*Anatomy of a Murder, Porgy and Bess, The Human Factor*), Nicholas Ray (*Johnny Guitar, Flying Leathernecks*), Vincente Minnelli (*Gigi, On a Clear Day You Can See Forever*), Anthony Mann (*The Man From Laramie, God's Little Acre*), John Ford (*The Grapes of Wrath, The Long Voyage Home*), Ernst Lubitsch (*Ninotchka*), all of the great filmmakers. Billy Wilder (*Sabrina, Some Like It Hot, The Front Page*) is another. He studied and appreciates all of their work.

HAVENS: *You guys share this love of film; do you feel like you too had some influence?*

PROFESSOR BASINGER: Oh, I don't know about that but we do share a love for film. He took a lot of classes with me. He was my teaching assistant. He worked for me on the film series helping me select the films. He is hugely committed to film here and very involved. I will always have extra screenings for students, who are interested in seeing certain types of films. People come and they are very devoted. But when it gets to be beautiful weather . . . in the spring everybody's out on the hill drinking beer. I'd open the door and there would be Joss, sitting in there by himself looking at *Johnny Guitar*.

HAVENS: *What do you think of the work he is doing now?*

PROFESSOR BASINGER: His work is a wonderful mixture of the greatest literature, music, ideas, movies, and works of art of all time. It's all mixed into his own mind and then he stirs it and adds his own original ideas that are then funneled out into this amazing work that is uniquely his.

He worries and frets over things. I admire him. I have to be careful about getting sentimental because he would hate that. The thing is he cares about what he does. He cares about being a good person. He's very private. I would never want to violate his privacy. He's a young man. What lies ahead as he grows and deepens . . . I can't even begin to think of what he is going to produce and how great it is going to be.

Thing is, Joss has a depth to his mythology and storytelling. We are watching a TV show initially on the WB, heaven help us. It is called *Buffy the Vampire Slayer* and I'm in my sixties and I'm crying when I'm watching it. What is that? It is one of the great mythic storytellers. It's more than just being a really successful, skilled, articulate filmmaker. There's something more to this. He's still so young and the thing is, he brings us pain in these stories as well as humor. In *Buffy* and *Angel* how you ricochet from laughing to being terrified to feeling like crying is astonishing. I think that's why you are writing a book about him, even though he's only in his mid-thirties. We all recognize there is something more here.

HAVENS: *Has success gone to his head in any way?*

PROFESSOR BASINGER: Having this huge success has not changed him at all except he has matured even more and deepened as a person. He's more thoughtful and caring. He's the same guy. The work is everything to him. Not the fame. It's all about doing the work. The guy is amazing. He can write five things at a time. It's astonishing what he does.

Joss the Script Doctor

2

". . . the final crappy humiliation of my crappy film career."

—Joss Whedon

Joss graduated from Wesleyan in 1987 determined to build a career in the movies. "I was sure I was too good for television," laughs Joss. "That's what my family did and I couldn't be bothered. I was a total snob. I never watched American TV, I only watched, like, *Masterpiece Theatre*. I was going to be a great independent filmmaker. The problem was, after school I had no idea how I was going to make it happen."

Joss set off for Los Angeles. He changed his name from Joe to Joss, the Chinese word for "luck." He lived with his father and worked on various experimental projects, such as a musical parody of the Oliver North hearings. He supported himself through work at the local video store and as a researcher at the Film Institute.

An aspiring filmmaker with waist-length bright red hair and eccentric points of view, Joss had some disastrous pitch meetings. Despite his trepidations and at his father's suggestion, he decided to try television. As Joss relates, "When I was just starting out, and I had no idea how I was going to become the brilliant independent filmmaker that I imagined myself to be, I thought, 'Well, I'll try my hand at a spec.' By selling a TV script, I could make enough money to sort of keep myself afloat. That was the first time I ever sat down and tried to write. I had never studied writing, or thought of myself as a writer exactly. I always assumed I would write whatever I made, but I never really gave it much thought. Then I sat down and really tried to write a script and found the great happiness of my life."

Writing turned out to be his true passion. It was like an addictive drug for Whedon. He poured everything he was and wanted to be into those early scripts. All the stories that had been rolling around in his brain for the first twenty years of his life were actually something he could put on paper. He began writing scripts at an amazing rate.

> Then I sat down and really tried to write a script and found the great happiness of my life. —Joss

He began sending scripts to everyone he knew in Hollywood, including some of his father's friends. The quality of his writing attracted notice from the beginning. Producer Howard Adler saw some of these early spec scripts. "It was his sense of humor I remember most," Adler says. "You don't forget something like that. By the time I tried to call and get him to come and work for me he was already working somewhere else. But he was definitely someone I really wanted on my staff."

Joss wound up taking a job as staff writer on the popular ABC television series *Roseanne*. The *Roseanne* work environment was famously difficult. Roseanne ran the show with an iron but erratic fist. She was notoriously challenging to work with and she changed producers and writers with alarming frequency. Conflict with management was continual, and the politics were fierce. Even she has admitted that she wasn't the easiest person to work with.

"You know I did a lot of crazy things back then, but I'm not going to apologize for it," said Roseanne after a press conference with television critics. "It was my show and I wanted to

Roseanne Barr, a funny lady but a tough boss.

make it my way. I worked with some great people, but there were a lot of them that had no business being in television. It's tough, and if you can't take it, well that's too damn bad."

But the chaos worked for Joss, at least at first. He was too junior to bear the brunt of Roseanne's difficult personality, and, most important, he got to write. In the first six months on the show he wrote five scripts, unheard of for a lowly staff writer. The frenetic pace suited his writing style and he was one of the few people there who liked having the pressure to churn out script after script. But the politics shifted and in the second half of the year he was shut out by the producers and had little to do.

It was around this time that Joss married Kai Cole, an interior designer. He describes her as "the funniest woman I've ever met" and jokes that he married her despite the fact that she was happy and popular in high school. Kai Cole would become an important part of Joss's life, influencing his life and work. A number of scenes in Buffy came from Kai's experiences. "[One example] in particular is the scene where they bring home Dawn when she was a baby. My wife was eight when they brought home her sister Dawn and it was on her birthday, which everyone forgot. So she was all cranky about it. They put Dawn in her arms, and she told me about this. She said she just felt like, 'I have to take care of this.' And so that whole scene was based on that story that she told me. I have a stepsister but I don't have a younger sister and I don't have the same kind of relationship with my family or siblings that she does. She has been very instrumental. There have been a lot of other things, but that in particular was just one thing I entirely stole."

But Joss didn't let his romance interfere with his work. He was using his free time at *Roseanne* to work on his script for the film that would later become *Buffy the Vampire Slayer*. He even worked on it during his honeymoon.

It was great to have the time to work on his script but Whedon, ever the workaholic, couldn't stand being on the payroll without being able to make a significant contribution. He left *Roseanne* after a year.

"I know people want me to say bad things about working there, but the truth is they gave me a shot when no one else would," Whedon says of working on the television show. "It was a strange place to work, but I had a chance to write scripts. Do you know how many writers are out there who never have a chance to do something like that? A lot of my stuff was rewritten, but it didn't matter. It was great experience for me."

Even though he was still determined to go into film, it wasn't long after quitting *Roseanne* that Whedon ended up on the short-lived television series *Parenthood*. While the show had some critical acclaim, it never did well in the ratings. For Whedon it was a chance to work with a talented writing staff and he made the most of the experience during his short time with the show.

"That was where I learned a lot about the creative side of writing for TV. It was another good experience for me and there were some great people who worked on that show."

His *Buffy* script complete, Whedon began pitching it to the studios. He received favorable comments but no one was willing to take a chance on such an unusual script by an unknown screenwriter. Most of the executives who rejected the script thought it was entertaining but didn't think there would be an audience.

"Everyone liked the script and I had a lot of encouragement, but no one wanted to pick it up," says Whedon. But the quality of the script, and the work he had done on *Roseanne* and *Parenthood,* earned him a modest reputation as a fast, reliable, and high-quality writer. He began getting small writing assignments.

One of Whedon's early film jobs was writing loop lines for movies that had already been made. The job entailed creating a joke or some type of conversation that would help the viewer make a connection between the scenes. Whedon wrote for the Kim Basinger and Alec Baldwin film *The Getaway* and the Sharon Stone and Gene Hackman film *The Quick and the Dead*, among others. Soon he would get larger and more lucrative script assignments, and ultimately become one of the most important script doctors in Hollywood. But early in his script-doctor career came his big break–*Buffy* was picked up.

> I wanted, just once, for her to fight back when the monster attacked, and kick his ass. —Joss

Joss had a powerful vision for *Buffy*. It was a concept he'd been thinking about for a long time. It began with a revisionist perspective on the countless horror-film scenes in which a young blond girl is pursued and ultimately killed by some hideous creature. In Joss's film the young woman would not be helpless. She would be the hunter instead of the victim.

"The idea for the film came from seeing too many blondes walking into dark alleyways and being killed," says Whedon. "I wanted, just once, for her to fight back when the monster attacked, and kick his ass. It was a simple thing for me to write because I knew exactly how I wanted things to work. I wanted her to have special powers and I thought it would be great to have vampires as the villains. She wouldn't be able to fit into normal society because she had these powers and this job that kept her from being what she wanted to be."

Joss's vision included the integration of elements rarely seen together—horror, action, comedy, and heart-wrenching emotion. In 1988 Joss optioned the script to Sandollar Productions, a production company founded by Dolly Parton and her manager, Sandy Gallin. Almost three years later, in 1991, Sandollar offered the script to Kaz and Fran Rubel Kuzui. They agreed to take on the film, provided Fran Kuzui could direct.

"The instant I saw the title, I knew this was a film I had to make," Fran says. "Five pages into the script and I was hooked. The more I read, the more I was attracted to the world that Joss Whedon had created. Here's a girl, a high school cheerleader, who's suddenly being told she's part of something else."

The Kuzuis were able to sell the concept to 20th Century-Fox, who funded the $9 million picture in exchange for worldwide rights. *Buffy* would become a reality and would be distributed by a major studio. Joss was thrilled. But his excitement soon turned to vexation and then horror as the production proceeded. What Joss discovered was how painful it was to have other people meddling with, and, from his perspective, destroying, his creations.

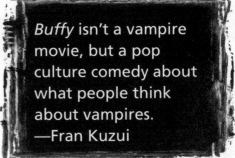

Buffy isn't a vampire movie, but a pop culture comedy about what people think about vampires.
—Fran Kuzui

In fairness to Joss, it's pretty clear that Fran Kuzui had an unusual interpretation of Joss's script. As she tells it, *Buffy* "isn't a vampire movie, but a pop culture comedy about what people think about vampires." Emphasizing the comedy at the expense of horror or genuine emotion, Kuzui created a very mediocre film. But observant critics noted the first-rate script that underlay the third-rate film. James Brundage of filmcritic.com noted that "the performances, admittedly, are lacking. The direction is downright bad . . . but all of this is made up in spades with one of the most finely crafted formula scripts courtesy of Joss Whedon." The *Fort Worth Star Telegram* stated that Whedon's "script [was] too witty for director Kuzui's dreary handling." *Time* magazine declared that Kuzui's "frenzied mistrust of her material is almost total."

> Whedon's script [was] too witty for director Kuzui's dreary handling.
> —*Fort Worth Star Telegram*

Like a slowly developing horror movie, Joss observed the gradual degradation of his script over the course of the filming. There were days when Whedon didn't want to go near the set because he feared the worst. His hip, scary script had been turned into a silly, campy film. There was nothing he could do about the miscasting or the rewriting.

SIMON BRANDLER

Kristy Swanson, the original Buffy.

The film starred Kristy Swanson, Donald Sutherland, Luke Perry, Rutger Hauer, and Paul Reubens. The casting was problematic. The two most experienced actors in the film, Donald Sutherland and Rutger Hauer, were extremely difficult. Sutherland played Merrick Jamison Smythe, the watcher in the film. He walked through his role with apparent contempt for the production and the script, often coming in with his lines rewritten. He was rude to the rest of the cast and certainly wanted nothing to do with the writer. Whedon said several times that working with Sutherland was one of the worst experiences of his life.

Rutger Hauer, the vampire Lothos, was difficult and bizarre. He insisted, for example, that he play a bedroom scene with Kristy Swanson in the

Paul Reubens was probably Whedon's favorite of the cast of the *Buffy* movie.

nude (he ultimately relented, at Swanson's request). But there were some bright moments. Whedon had a great appreciation for Paul Reubens (Amilyn) before the film, but even more so after.

"He knew instinctively what needed to be done with his character and it stands out in the film," says Whedon. "He's such a great guy and at the same time he's never afraid to push through boundaries. I appreciated him a great deal at that time as a performer and as a human being. He was nice to everyone and professional. But he never took himself too seriously."

But Reubens's performance, which was critically praised, was not enough to save the film. Most damaging of all was Kuzui's "pop culture" interpretation of the script. At the time Whedon simply said, "I don't understand that approach." Years later he was more blunt: "The director ruined it."

"What I started with was a horror action comedy. It had fright, it had camera movement, it had acting–all kinds of interesting things that weren't in the final film. Apart from the jokes–and there were a lot more of them [in my script] and all of my favorite ones got cut–it was supposed to have a little more edge to it. It was supposed to be a visceral entertainment rather than a glorified sitcom where everyone pretty much stands in front of the camera, says their joke, and exits. I wasn't happy about anything. I had one advantage from it: the direction was so bland that the jokes kind of stood out, because they were the only things to latch on to. In a way, that kind of worked for me because it got people to notice it. But that was a big disappointment to me.

> I knew in the future that I would find a way to do things in a different way. —Joss

"It was crushing," adds Whedon. "I had written this scary film about an empowered woman, and they turned it into a broad comedy. It was terrible and a great lesson for me. I knew in the future that I would find a way to do things in a different way."

As it turns out, Joss was to learn this lesson many times over.

Disappointed and upset by *Buffy*, Whedon returned to his scriptwriting career. The quality of the *Buffy* script had not escaped Hollywood producers, and his ability to rapidly produce high-quality work impressed the studios. So Joss entered the world of the elite script doctor. He was soon working on *Speed*, *Toy Story*, *Waterworld*, *Twister*, and *Alien Resurrection*. The work was extremely lucrative, with Joss making $100,000 *per week* on certain assignments. But for Joss, who measured his worth by the quality of his writing and how well it was translated to the screen, it was frustrating and unsatisfying.

According to Joss, "[Script doctoring is] fun and lucrative. But it's like eating candy all day. It tastes great but it is not very filling. You want to create something from beginning to end, but working on these movies is like solving a puzzle. We have all pieces–here's the stunts and all the story, now make it make sense. Make the people's emotions make sense. Make it funny, real, and like it's actually happening. It's fun but not creative."

"You know what it is," says producer and creator David E. Kelley (*The Practice*, *Boston Public*, *Ally McBeal*, *Lake Placid*), "you have this great vision when you write a script and then by the time you see it on screen it is about as far from that vision as it can get. When I wrote *Mystery, Alaska*, from the time I turned it in, it probably went through a hundred rewrites, and that's not an exaggeration. Everyone has their ideas of what it should be and your vision is lost in the process. That's why I'm sticking with television for now. I don't have to listen to anyone but the network, and they let me do my own thing most of the time."

Despite the excellent compensation, a Hollywood scriptwriter is a low man on the totem pole, and much of his work–sometimes all of his work–is not used. "Sometimes they bring you in to fix a few lines or sometimes it's the entire film. People give me credit for writing these scripts and the truth is, most of what I wrote never made it to the screen," says Whedon. "It's a strange business, and in many ways, though I didn't know it at the time, television was a much more forgiving world to work in. When you write a film, there are too many people who can take what you do and make it into something which is the opposite of what you wrote."

Joss's appreciation of his script-doctor role was directly related to his opinion of the underlying story and how much creative freedom he had in writing the final script. The most frustrating situation was when the underlying story was weak. "I've been pitched ideas, or seen scripts, where I've been like, 'You don't need me. You need to [shouting] *not make this*.' There have been some terrible ones. But the thing is, for a script doctor, the best thing in the world is a good idea with a terrible script. Assuming they'll let you play with it, which they did on *Toy Story*. Because you have the solid structure, and you can work the story into it."

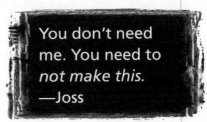

You don't need me. You need to *not make this*. —Joss

Joss moved to the next level in his career when his agent, Chris Harbert of United Talent Agency, landed him the job of rewriting the script for *Speed*. Whedon got the assignment, in part, by agreeing to take on the ten-week project for a mere $150,000. While not much by the standards of the top script doctors, this was serious money for Joss.

Working on *Speed* was one of Joss's best experiences as a script doctor. He loved the story and he had full freedom to rewrite the dialogue, although he couldn't change any stunts. "Apart from rewriting about 90 percent of the dialogue on *Speed*, the best work was the stuff that nobody would ever notice: just trying to make the whole thing track logically and emotionally so that all of those insane and over-the-top stunts–one after the other–would make sense," says Joss. "That's the part of script doctoring that's actually interesting to me. When somebody says, 'We've got a guy and he's falling off a cliff, and later he's hanging from a helicopter and we need you to tell us why. We need you to make the audience believe he's doing it.' That's what *Speed* was."

ALBERT L. ORTEGA

Joss lets Keanu Reeves shine in *Speed*.

Speed was a tremendous commercial success. It was an adrenaline rush and was dubbed "*Die Hard* on a Bus" and "*Die Hard* Without the Slow Parts." But a few critics noticed, amidst the action, the clever dialogue and wonderfully developed relationship between the characters played by Keanu Reeves and Sandra Bullock. Roger Ebert of the *Chicago Sun-Times* noted that "[Reeves] and Bullock have good chemistry; they appreciate the humor that is always flickering just beneath the surface of the preposterous plot. And Hopper's dialogue has been twisted into savagely ironic understatements that provide their own form of comic relief." Peter Travis of *Rolling Stone* observed that "the fireworks wouldn't count for much if the hardware overwhelmed the humanity. *Speed* cinches its spot as the thrill ride of summer by providing characters to hiss at and root for. Jack and Annie actually manage to strike up a convincing romance even at hyperspeed and without taking their eyes off the road. It's an impressive feat . . ."

Whedon landed another plum job on *Toy Story*, where he was one of seven writers. It was the perfect opportunity for Joss because "it was a great idea, with a script I didn't like at all." It was Whedon's hand at the script that brought many of the funniest jokes, and the toys that told them, to life. At the end of the movie the audience was emotionally invested in the characters and the story and that was what the young writer had hoped would happen.

Toy Story wasn't without its troubles. Being one of seven credited writers (one of whom was the director) was not a recipe for creative freedom. And some of Joss's funniest jokes didn't get past the Disney bureaucracy, including one in which Mr. Potato Head takes off one of his eyes and discretely rolls it under Bo Peep's skirt.

Toy Story was a commercial and critical success. Once again, observant critics noted the quality of the writing. Kenneth Turan of the *LA Times* declared that "when a film has seven writers, it's not a positive sign, but *Toy Story* turns out to be smart fun on a verbal as well as visual level." Barbara Shulgasser of the *San Francisco Examiner* declared that "what makes this movie so delightful is a solid story line (which has always been Disney's strength) and terrific dialogue written by Joss Whedon, Andrew Stanton, Joel Cohen, and Alec Sokolow."

Toy Story was nominated for an Academy Award for Best Original Screenplay. "I'm not sure it's something you ever get used to," says Whedon of being nominated. "I was happy that the film did well, and it showed that we could do something a little different and get away with it. I thought it was a really sweet film and it definitely showed a different side of me. There were some darker aspects to it, but for the most part it was a light, enjoyable film."

Joss soon landed a six-figure-per-week assignment as a script doctor for *Waterworld*. It was an unqualified disaster. Beyond the embarrassment of his association with a well-publicized failure, he felt the creative frustration of failing to create a script he felt good about. "On *Waterworld*, I lost the patient," Whedon confesses. "By the time I got there, there was too much going on for me to make a real difference. They were too far into it . . . there were only tiny cracks I could get in between. I will tell you that *Waterworld* is one of the projects that proved to me that the higher you climb, the worse the view."

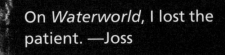

On *Waterworld*, I lost the patient. —Joss

Joss's frustration with *Waterworld* soon faded as he received the chance of a lifetime. He was asked to write the script for *Alien 4*, an opportunity he had dreamed about since he first saw *Alien* when he was fourteen. But once again, what should have been a happy experience became a nightmare and almost soured him forever on the movie business.

When he was first asked to write the next *Alien* saga, Joss didn't hesitate. *Alien* was "sacred text" and Joss couldn't turn it down. Enthralled with *Alien* and *Aliens*, Whedon felt (as many did) that *Alien 3* was a disappointment. "I think the fans were robbed in the third one. They actually had a scene where people we didn't know were killed by the alien. That's Jason, that's bullshit, because nothing is more boring than people you don't know being killed. [*Alien 3*] was beautiful but it was neither exciting nor scary, which is a travesty. . . . I just want every scene to contain something amazing. I want to do *Evil Dead* where it's menacing, and then about twenty minutes into it the action starts and never stops."

[*Alien 3*] was beautiful but it was neither exciting nor scary, which is a travesty. . . . —Joss

Joss was given a golden opportunity to change the future of the *Alien* franchise by writing a script that would put it on the path to glory once again. Initially, 20th Century-Fox wasn't sure they could get Sigourney Weaver to play the role of Ripley again. So Joss was asked to write the script without Ripley who, after all, had died at the end of *Alien 3*. He banged out a script without Ripley and was pleased with the result.

A few months later the studio panicked, worrying that they wouldn't be able to generate the box-office success they needed without Weaver. They made her a deal she couldn't refuse and asked Joss to go back to the drawing board. Joss initially rebelled, thinking, "bullshit, she's dead," but came around to thinking that reviving Ripley could be very powerful. But, much as he tried to do in season six of *Buffy*, Joss wanted to make her resurrection real, and not without a price.

"We're not just saying, 'We've brought her back, let's make the movie.' It's the central issue of the movie, the fact that we bring her back. We know that once you do that, everything must be different. When somebody comes back from the dead, especially in a movie where death is the ultimate threat, you can't just say 'It's okay, anybody can die and come back.' It's very important to me that it's a very tortuous, grotesque process so that people will viscerally feel what it's like to be horribly reborn in a lab. And then the whole question of what is she is raised. Is she human? Has she changed? There is the factor that she was pregnant with an alien. Is she all woman? Is there a little something wrong there? There are a lot of issues."

There was some wonderful writing and a number of compelling scenes in *Alien Resurrection*, in particular the scene where Ripley discovers the remains of earlier attempts to clone her. The Ripley character is complex and subtle; she is uncertain of who she is and where her loyalties lie–and so are we. In *Alien Resurrection*, Weaver was given the opportunity to really stretch herself in portraying the reborn, part-alien Ripley. And leave it to Whedon to transform superheroine Ripley into a character many times tougher than the original!

Alien Resurrection did well in the box office while receiving mixed reviews from critics. But the harshest criticism of the movie came from Whedon himself, who felt the director had ruined an excellent script. "I liked the script for *Alien Resurrection*," he explained. "But the movie? I . . . hated it. I thought it was as badly directed as a movie could be and I thought it was bad in ways that I didn't know movies could be bad. I learned more from that movie than anything I've ever been involved in. I thought it was badly cast and badly shot. I didn't like the production design. Everything that was wrong in the script was incredibly highlighted by it, and everything that was right about the script was squashed, with one or two very minor exceptions. I just couldn't believe how much I hated it. I wasn't really involved in production. I went to dailies once and thought, 'This doesn't seem right, but I'm sure it's fine.' I saw the director's cut with the studio brass and I actually began to cry. Then I started to put on a brave face and tried to be a team player, because Fox is

Sigourney Weaver returns for *Alien Resurrection*, a low point in Joss's film career.

my home. But I feel enough time has passed; it's out on video and I can say with impunity that I was just shattered by how crappy it was.

"I really had high hopes for it," he added. "I worked really hard on it for a really long time. But you know what? It was an epiphany; a wake-up call. After that I said, 'The next person who ruins one of my scripts is going to be me.' I have always wanted to direct. I'm not just a bitter writer trying to protect his shit. I think they're two very different talents, but there is an element of 'Enough already!' It really drives home the argument of why television is so much more satisfying. It was the final crappy humiliation of my crappy film career."

Whedon was now determined to find a venue that would give him more control. But he was painfully aware that while he was clearly being recognized for his talents as a writer, he was still best known

> I saw the director's cut with the studio brass and I actually began to cry. —Joss

for his *Buffy* movie script. As he said a few years earlier, "I'm still 'Joss *Buffy the Vampire Slayer* Whedon,' which is really depressing."

Ironically, it was *Buffy* itself and Joss's reputation as the creator of *Buffy* that would give him his first opportunity to realize the creative control he craved.

Buffy: Round Two

3

"My wife, at the premiere [of *Buffy*], was sort of like, 'Well, you know honey, maybe in a few years you could make it again, the way you wanted to.' I went, 'Oh, ha ha, honey, that doesn't happen in Hollywood! You're so naive!' Well . . . it really doesn't."

"Somebody came along and kissed Sleeping Beauty Joss and said, 'You can have your dream back now.'"

—Joss Whedon

Joss was getting used to disappointment. Despite his successes as a screenwriter, despite the money and the growing recognition, very little of his creative output had made it to the screen intact, in a fashion that he could be proud of. Most disappointing of all was *Buffy*, in which he had invested so much of his heart and mind. But Joss would get a second chance at *Buffy* and the result would change his life.

Gail Berman, an executive with Sandollar Productions, decided that *Buffy the Vampire Slayer* would make a great television show. Berman believed the concept had great potential and, even more, she recognized the potential of Joss Whedon.

"There was something about that original script that made me believe there was much more to this guy and his vampire slayer than any of us could have imagined," says Berman. "Joss is a genius, and given half a chance to show what he could do, I knew magic would happen. The script was fun with an edge. There wasn't anything else like it out there."

It took a bit of cajoling to get Joss to consider the TV possibilities for *Buffy*. Joss loved the movies. What he had dreamed about his whole life, what had crystallized for him at Wesleyan, was his passion for movies. The big time, the big money was in movies. Television was what his father and grandfather had done. He was determined not to simply follow in their footsteps.

But he wasn't happy. Despite the success he'd experienced as a screenwriter, he didn't feel satisfied. Everything he'd written had either been ruined on the screen or it had been changed enough so that it was no longer fully his work. Joss came to the realization that television might be able to give him what he craved–genuine creative control over the final product. "At the time I still wasn't ready to go back to television, but then I realized I'd have a lot more control if I did. I liked the idea that I would be in charge of every aspect of the show, and the only person I could blame if it failed was me."

At first the idea was to make *Buffy* into a half-hour children's show, a girl-power version of *Power Rangers*. Joss played with this idea, but soon realized he didn't want to do a *Buffy* that was silly or just for fun. He wanted to do *Buffy* for real, with powerful emotions and genuine horror. He wanted it dark.

So Joss set out to do a presentation film, sort of a mini-pilot. It included most of the cast that would ultimately star in *Buffy*, although the role of Willow was played by Riff Regan. Joss had never directed professionally before, but he had studied film for years and had a natural talent for creating powerful visuals. He had a strong script and he knew exactly what he wanted on screen. But he was given a weak crew and he didn't know how to effectively communicate with them. "I was a first-time guy who didn't know what he was doing, surrounded by old veterans who didn't know what they were doing," Joss complained. The result was pretty dreadful. But the power of the concept and the script came through. WB approved twelve episodes of *Buffy* as a midseason replacement on the fledgling network. No one knew at the time that *Buffy* would soon set the tone for the entire network.

From the beginning, the title was an obstacle. The network tried to get Whedon to change it from *Buffy the Vampire Slayer* to *Slayer,* but Joss was adamant. "I believe that anyone who isn't open to a show with this title isn't invited to the party. I made the title very specifically to say 'This is what it is.' It wears itself on its sleeve. It's sophomoric, it's silly, it's comedy-horror-action; it's all there in the title. Having the metaphor to work with makes the show better, and having the silly title makes the show cooler. At least to me."

> I believe that anyone who isn't open to a show with this title isn't invited to the party. —Joss

Essential to Joss's concept for *Buffy* was to take all of the misery of his high school years and put them into the series. "I don't know about you, but in high school I turned everything inside and it was all so horrible and dramatic. Everyone always says it's part of being a teen, but it isn't easy for anyone. It may be all those hormones; I'm not really sure but there's just so much emotion happening and nowhere to let them go. You blow everything out of proportion, and the tiniest thing can set you off. You have no control over the situations you are in, and that's something that we use in our show on a continuing basis. I don't care how together you are during that time of your life, everyone experiences those seesawing emotions. Puberty basically sucks."

> If you had asked me in the beginning if we were going to be a successful show, I would have told you that you are on smack.
> —Sarah Michelle Gellar

At the time of the launch, *Buffy*'s success was far from evident. In the world of network television, being a midseason replacement on the WB was pretty much the bottom. Joss had a small budget to work with, which made producing a quality show difficult, especially one that required special effects in every episode. "If you had asked me in the beginning if we were going to be a successful show, I would have told you that you are on smack," laughs Sarah Michelle Gellar. "I didn't think there was any way that people would get what we were doing. It was such genius but I was sure no one would watch."

Buffy's low status and limited budget made recruiting big-name talent almost impossible. But Joss turned out to have a knack for spotting talent and was able to hire an excellent writing and production team. Even more important, he attracted a team, especially writers, who had the potential to grow. Two of his early writers, Marti Noxon and David Greenwalt, would become executive producers of their own shows (Noxon would executive-produce *Buffy* in season five, and Greenwalt would executive-produce *Angel* from its launch).

When Noxon initially joined the *Buffy* team as a writer, she was thrilled to be part of a show with such a smart writing and high-quality team. But getting others to share her excitement wasn't as easy. "When I got this job, it was the first season I'd ever gone out for television work. I had been working on plays and stuff," says Noxon. "I called my mom to tell her that I got this job, and I was shaking with excitement. I called her from a pay phone, and there was this long pause, and she said, 'Oh, honey, next year you'll do better.'"

> I called my mom to tell her that I got this job, and I was shaking with excitement. I called her from a pay phone, and there was this long pause, and she said, 'Oh, honey, next year you'll do better.'
> —Marti Noxon

Joss's energy and vision attracted top people and motivated them to do their best work for him. He was able to attract a production, design, and special-effects team who were able to work miracles with a tiny budget.

"The thing is, you have to find the right people who can work together," says Whedon. "I've been on sets where there were too many egos and people weren't talking. The director can't deal with the actors and so on. It's ridiculous. Part of the control thing was finding a way that all of these people could work together on a happy set.

"The truth is they have all sold their souls to me," laughs Joss Whedon as he discusses his cast. It must be true, because Joss managed to attract a stellar cast and succeeded in keeping them working well together for seven years. His stars ranged from show business veterans (Gellar, Alyson Hannigan, Anthony Head) to relative newcomers (David Boreanaz, Nicholas Brendon), but each of them proved capable of powerful, nuanced performances. With the exception of secondary characters Eliza Dushku and Seth Green, both of whom he lost to the movies, Joss managed to keep all of his important actors in the fold, despite the fact that many of them were not regulars. (And Dushku returns to *Buffy* for a number of episodes in season seven).

Critical to the success of *Buffy* was finding the right actress to play the lead. Whedon knew exactly what he wanted. His Buffy needed to embody a complex mix of strength, vulnerability, sweetness, ruthlessness, beauty, and determination. The pretty young woman had to look like the innocent blonde who would be killed in the first act of a low-budget slasher film while being able to radiate an intensity that would give even the nastiest demon pause.

Whedon knew he was asking for a lot but he was determined not to compromise. He auditioned hundreds of women without finding what he was looking for. Sarah Michelle Gellar was one of these young women but he had her tagged to play Cordelia, a role not too different from her Emmy-winning role on the soap *All My Children*.

Gellar wasn't sure she wanted to play Cordelia, for fear of being typecast as the bitchy brunette. But she loved the script. "I sat back and I kept rereading the pilot, which I still have, and there was something so special and so unique about it. There just wasn't another show like it. And I said, 'I feel like I want to be a part of this.' There was something in the writing; there was something in the story."

So Gellar agreed to audition for Cordelia. Two auditions later, she won the role. But there was still no Buffy. The studio executives suggested to Whedon that he consider Gellar for the Buffy role. Gellar was told that she had won the role of Cordelia, but if she wanted, she could audition for the Buffy role. Gellar agreed. Joss had her audition many times, long, grueling auditions that took their toll. When asked to come back for a final time, Gellar broke down in tears. "Never mind, I'll just be Cordelia," she sobbed. When she did return, she found Joss and casting team there to congratulate her on winning the role of Buffy.

"I guess we did make it pretty tough on her," says Whedon. "But we knew that she was definitely the one."

"Auditions are scary things anyway," says Gellar. "You go in and often read for a different part than you eventually get. It's weird but they look at you and sometimes say, 'Hey, try reading this other role.' I really didn't have a clue after going back and forth to the auditions where I was with them. I think they try really hard not to let you know if they like you, because there's some morbid fascination with the desperation these poor actresses feel. I do know that when I heard I finally had the part, I felt like I'd earned it in more ways than one."

> I think they try really hard not to let you know if they like you, because there's some morbid fascination with the desperation these poor actresses feel.
> —Sarah Michelle Gellar

The role of Buffy would turn Gellar into a star. But that was far from evident at the time and her new role didn't impress her friends. "You try being on a midseason replacement show on the WB called *Buffy the Vampire Slayer* and see how much respect you get," Gellar explains.

Gellar would turn out to be the ideal choice for the series, casually beautiful, credibly tough, and genuinely funny. Most critically, she brought a powerful vulnerability to Buffy's superhero persona. "I wanted to stress her vulnerability, because she came off a little harsh in the movie," Joss explains. "I wanted to pull back from that. This is someone who has already been a slayer. You want to make her an underdog. She is stronger than everyone around her, because she is faster and smarter. So you need to have that empathy that everybody puts on her."

Buffy was far from Gellar's first role. At nineteen, Gellar was a show-business veteran, having played Kendall Hart on the ABC soap opera *All My Children* from 1993 to 1995. She also played several small roles in various television shows and miniseries throughout the early nineties, from *Swans Crossing* to *Girl Talk* with Soleil Moon Frye.

When she left her popular role as Kendall on *All My Children*, Gellar's fans and a few of her peers thought she was foolish to leave such a plum job. But ongoing conflict with Susan Lucci made the work environment stressful, so Gellar decided it was time for the next phase in her career. She packed her bags and moved from New York to California with her mother. There were regular auditions after arriving, but nothing worked out. Trudging off to auditions was a daily event, and while her savings could keep her going for a short time, Gellar knew she had to find work fast. She wasn't sure what to think when the script for *Buffy the Vampire Slayer* arrived.

"The title would throw anyone off," laughs Gellar. "But in that first script you could see that this was a strong female character and those aren't always easy to find. I knew going in that it would be a very physical role, but in hindsight I didn't really have a clue what I was in for."

Gellar could relate to what Buffy was going through. The actress, who was born and grew up in Manhattan, had many of the same high school conflicts as the characters in *Buffy*. "I was an actor and I tried to go to a high school where that's what you trained for, but they didn't like the fact that I was already working," says Gellar. "They weren't very happy about any of that. And I never fit in. I don't know if it was jealousy or if it was because I was never there, but I always felt like such an outsider."

In one of their first interviews in front of the press, Whedon was incredulous when the beautiful Gellar mentioned that she felt like a geek in high school.

"Does anyone have a good time in high school?" laughed Gellar. "I felt like a total geek and didn't fit in at all."

"Are you serious?" asked Whedon. "You have to be kidding."

"I am not!" said Gellar seriously. "High school was not a fun time in my life and I did feel like a total geek most of the time. I didn't have any friends."

"Wow," Whedon said. "See, that's what I mean about this being so universal. There are millions of people who had horrible high school experiences and we can all relate to Buffy in some way."

Secrets of Success

4

"[When asked, 'What's your secret for building a cult phenomenon?'] . . . I'm not telling you. That's all I've got."

"I have never had any particular life of my own, so I don't see any particular reason why anyone should run out to get one. Of course, if they're dressing up like Willow and staying in their basement for nine months at a time, that's not good. But the show's designed to foster slavish devotion; it has it from me, and I entirely respect it in others."

—Joss Whedon

Whedon launched *Buffy* with grand ambition. Knowing full well *Buffy*'s status as an obscure show on a new network, with a tiny budget and a minimal network commitment, Joss set out to build an empire. Joss envisioned *Buffy* as a genuine cultural phenomenon, complete with action figures and comic strips, cartoons and spin-offs. Joss kept this to himself because he knew how crazy it made him seem. But he was deadly serious and, against all odds, he made it happen.

It's easy to underestimate the size and devotion of the *Buffy* fan community. *Buffy* has often been among the top ten searches on leading search engines and is frequently the most populated Internet discussion group of any television show. Literally hundreds of *Buffy* fan sites have been created by enthusiastic fans, covering everything from slash fiction to homages to minor characters. So, how did he do it?

Joss succeeded because he very deliberately introduced to *Buffy* seven key ingredients that had never been brought together in a television show before. Combined, these seven ingredients created a show that is truly unique and genuinely precious.

Mixing up the Genres

First, Joss set out to create a truly cross-genre show. Essential to the concept of *Buffy the Vampire Slayer* was that it would integrate four distinct genres—horror, action, comedy, and drama. Some combination of these genres was part of the best television shows—serious dramas lightened with moments of comedy, or comedies spiced with an element of action. A few shows, notably *NYPD Blue*, integrated drama, action, and comedy. But *Buffy* was unique in integrating all four genres and giving each of them equal weight. Is *Buffy* a comedy or a drama? Action or horror? There is no real answer to this question, because *Buffy* is, at heart, all four of these.

This integration lies at the core of *Buffy's* appeal, but it made the show almost impossible to describe in a way that movie and network executives understood. How do you sell a show that doesn't fall into a clear genre? For this reason, the movie version of *Buffy* was turned into a comedy, much to Joss's dismay. As a television show, *Buffy* was rejected by the major networks. Ultimately, the fledgling WB accepted *Buffy* as a cross-genre show. This acceptance was either a result of WB's vision or of its executives' inexperience. But the reality is that it's unlikely *Buffy* would have been allowed to proceed with its cross-genre approach on one of the more established networks.

Integrating these genres made great demands on the writers, but it also required highly skilled directors and a strong technical crew. Horror, for example, demands different framing and lighting than comedy or action. Horror is fundamentally about the loss of control; the main characters don't control the action, can't take the initiative. The action, instead, is controlled by the villain. A good director creates a mood consistent with this loss of control, with plenty of tight shots and deep shadows. Action is almost the opposite; it's about taking control. In action, the main characters take the initiative and drive the plot, requiring a very different mood. It's a rare director that can integrate these elements well, and shift rapidly between them.

Continuity

The second ingredient that led to *Buffy*'s cult status was the incredible degree of continuity Whedon built into the series. The most obvious aspect of this continuity was the season-long story arcs, which allowed complex plots that fans could sink their teeth into. Unlike soaps, Joss did not write the show as a seemingly never-ending series of plot developments. Instead, Whedon followed the lead of his favorite author, Charles Dickens, who planned out his novels in their entirety but wrote and published each chapter separately. Joss knew exactly where he was going. He created a story arc with a clear beginning, middle, and end, that stretched over the twenty-two episodes of the series.

Whedon assumes that his viewers know everything that has happened on the series to date and he makes sure his characters remember what's happened as well. Television shows that miss this drive him crazy. On *The X-Files*, for instance, Scully's skepticism persisted despite weekly evidence of the paranormal. "You're an idiot," Joss laughs, referring to Scully, "it's a monster."

But Whedon went beyond complex season-long plots to bring unprecedented continuity to the entire run of the series. As a fan himself, Joss knew how fans obsess over shows and take note of every detail. So he obsessed over the details himself, providing a degree of continuity which was unnoticed by most viewers, but which rewarded his fans and increased their loyalty. Examples of these continuities are legion. In "Restless," the finale of season four, Joss put Willow back into the "softer side of Sears" outfit she wore in the first episode. After Joyce's death, we see Giles mourning while listening to Cream's "Tales of Brave Ulysses," the same song he played the night he and Joyce had sex. Sometimes the continuity takes a turn towards the ludicrous, as when Giles and Buffy recount the number of times she's saved the world in "The Gift." But overall, the continuity is a pleasure for fans of the show.

Even more enticing to the attentive fan is *Buffy*'s foreshadowing. Because Joss plans his major plot points years in advance, he is able to tantalize viewers with hints of what's to come. A wonderful example of this is found in the dream sequence in "Graduation Day, Part II." Faith tells Buffy, "Oh yeah. Miles to go. Little Miss Muffet counting down from seven three oh." The numbers were referenced again in the season four finale, "Restless," when Buffy noted that the time was 7:30. "Some fans figured it out," Whedon said. "Seven three oh is exactly two years in days. Two years until the next climax. Whatever she's talking about will be resolved." This climax turns out to be Buffy's death at the end of season five.

> Oh yeah. Miles to go. Little Miss Muffet counting down from seven three oh.
> —Faith

One critical aspect of continuity is the recognition that time passes and a willingness to allow the characters to grow and evolve in unforeseen ways. This is risky, because the evolution might not please fans. Most television shows do everything they can to adhere to the formula that made them successful in the first place. *Buffy*, on the other hand, is continually taking risks. Joss understands that this is part of the show's appeal.

The key, Joss believes, is for the writers, the viewers, and the characters all to be worried about the same things. When Angel left the show, for example, the writers and the fans worried about Buffy. Will she ever find another love? Could any future lover be as worthy as Angel? These worries are fine, Joss feels, because these are the exact concerns Buffy has. Similarly, when the Scoobies left high school, viewers and writers worried about the continued appeal of the show. But, again, these concerns echo those of the characters—will life be as good after high school?

Carpe Diem

The flip side of Joss's commitment to continuity is his opportunism. Joss's ability to seize opportunities is the third critical ingredient to *Buffy*'s success. Joss's talents are well suited for television, because he has the ability to grasp opportunities that present themselves and work them into the overall plot of each season. While Joss is famous for killing beloved characters, he equally often saves characters slated for death who display unexpected appeal. Darla was slated to be killed by Willow at the end of the second episode of the first season. Spike was similarly killed off in the original scripts. But in both cases Joss liked what he saw enough to make last-minute changes that saved some of the show's most popular characters.

Joss is a careful observer of how his actors are being perceived. He found that Hannigan's Willow had a special vulnerability and that when she was put in jeopardy it "opens your heart." So he arranged to have her put in jeopardy at key points in the story arc of each season. Similarly, Joss knew he had a winner when he observed Gellar's performance when she finds she is destined to die at the end of season one. Buffy would have many heart-wrenching events in future episodes, to say the least.

Joss also found that opportunistic moves were forced upon him. "You have to stay fluid because television is a fluid medium," Joss explains. "There are times when you might lose an actor. That gives you an opportunity to make changes that might not have otherwise happened. When we lost Oz because Seth Green wanted to go off and make movies, it gave a chance to bring in Amber who turned out to be a wonderful addition to our show. That's the upside of keeping things fluid. But you have to have those basic story arcs down and move people in and out of them."

Joss cleverly leaves room for opportunities to develop. He tries to avoid saying too much about a character's background, so that he can work something new in if an idea emerges. This allowed the writers, for example, to decide that Jenny Calendar was actually a gypsy (and a double agent) in the middle of season two.

Loving the Fans

The fourth ingredient to *Buffy*'s success is its ability to stay in touch with fan sensibilities. Whedon trusts his instincts regarding what works, but at the same time he is very interested in fan reaction and takes fans seriously. Many television writers create the impression that they consider themselves a lot smarter than the folks they are writing for. This is never true with Joss, who credits fans with being smart and paying attention. He relates to fans and considers himself one of them. When asked about William Shatner's joking statement that fans should "get a life," Whedon responded, "I have never had any particular life of my

Seth Green, a mainstay in seasons two and three, has moved on to a movie career, including the *Austin Powers* films.

own, so I don't see any particular reason why anyone should run out to get one. Of course, if they're dressing up like Willow and staying in their basement for nine months at a time, that's not good. But the show's designed to foster slavish devotion; it has it from me, and I entirely respect it in others."

When fans seemed to reject Oz, for example, Whedon responded by giving them a scene designed to bring him into their hearts. This is the van scene in "Innocence," where Oz declines to kiss Willow, stating that "Well, to the casual observer, it would appear that you're trying to make your friend Xander jealous or even the score or something. And that's on the empty side . . . See, in my fantasy, when I'm kissing you, you're kissing me. It's okay. I can wait." The viewer can see Willow falling in love with Oz as he says this and, as Joss planned, the audience falls in love with Oz as well.

But this doesn't mean he gives fans what they want. Whedon takes an almost perverse pride in horrifying fans. Over and over he kills the characters they love, including Ms. Calendar in season two, Joyce in season five, Tara in season six, and Doyle in season one of *Angel*. Joss considers the outcry a sign that he's doing well. "I need to give them what they need, not what they want. They need to have their hearts broken. They need to see change. They hated Oz, and then they hated that he left. These things are inevitable. . . . If people don't care when you killed off a great character, then you haven't done it right," says Whedon. "When you are writing a horror show, it's a given that your same group of people, no matter what situation they find themselves, are going to be back for the next episode. It's good now and then to shake things up."

Joss uses the Internet as a vehicle to keep his fingers on the pulse of fan sentiment. He claims to be the furthest thing from a techie, saying "I sort of came to it late. I don't need it much in my life; I haven't mastered it. My

Joss with Nicholas Brendon and Alyson Hannigan, entertaining fans at the Los Angeles comic convention.

wife is very proficient. I'm still at 'What's download?'" But his lack of knowledge hasn't stopped him from spending considerable time on message boards interacting with fans or just lurking and learning. He recognizes how helpful the Internet has been to the show's development.

His cast recognizes it as well. "I don't think we'd be here if it wasn't for the Net," states Sarah Michelle Gellar. "It was the Internet that really kicked us off, because that's where this loyal fan base could get together and spread the word."

> I'm still at 'What's download?' —

But while Joss mostly appreciates and enjoys his interactions with fans on the Internet, it's not without its frustrations. The Internet makes keeping secrets very difficult, and more than once Joss has found future plot points revealed in cyberspace. "I like being surprised and I want the audience to feel the same way," says Whedon. "It's getting tougher with the Internet to keep things secret, but we are doing our best."

Joss works hard to keep his plot twists secret, which sometimes means not sharing them with the cast too early. "And in this scene you're gay, and action," laughs Whedon about how the actors sometimes

> I don't think we'd be here if it wasn't for the Net.
> —Sarah Michelle Gellar

receive their lines at the last minute. "Sometimes I don't know until late in the game, and it sort of blossoms and I go, 'Oh my God, this is going on . . . so we are going to shift to here or were going to send it in this direction.' But I do generally keep them posted on the big things. I told Kristine she was going to die like two years before, so she was prepared. That was probably one of the toughest ones we had to do, because we knew what was coming. She was one of the favorites around here and we still miss her."

And in this scene you're gay, and action. —Joss

Joss has also found that casual statements (or jokes) made on the Internet are taken with deadly seriousness by some fans. This concerned him at first, but in the end he decided to have fun with it, at least judging from this post:

"The truth is, I was a little wigged by all the commotion my posting caused. I think the worst thing that could happen would be for the Willow/Tara storyline to become some kind of publicity stunt. I guess if I type something here, the papers are gonna pick up on it, and there's nothing I can do about it. So I'd like to make the following announcements:

1. FROM NOW ON, EVERYONE ON BUFFY WILL BE GAY. You heard it here first. And not just a little gay, either. Whole new show.
2. MATT DAMON: MONSTER FIGHTER. Yes, a multi-episode arc feature the talented Mr. Damon and look for some of his movie star friends to make "monstrous" cameos!
3. FREE PRESENTS AND MONEY for everyone who tunes in. Swear to God.
4. NUDITY, NUDITY, NUDITY.
5. NAKEDNESS.
6. ZEPPLIN FIGHT OVER NEPTUNE! Just in time for sweeps, the gang is going to have an "out of this world" adventure with wacky Xander at the controls! This episode is budgeted at 18 million dollars, and will change history.

Okay! Well, I'll just settle back and let the publicity come rolling in. Yep, ratings are bound to soar once everyone gets wind of the exciting and controversial direction I'm taking the show in. In the meanwhile, I hope you, the fans, enjoy the all-nude, all-gay Buffy. It's gonna be a hoot!"

Keeping It Real

The fifth element of *Buffy*'s success is its relentless reality. More than one critic has noted the irony that the most realistic show on television is a vampire fantasy. *Buffy* paints complex, interesting characters and makes a point of avoiding stereotypes. They are continually evolving and growing and fans come to feel that they not only know the characters, they know where they've come from.

Joss has famously said that "there will never be a very special *Buffy*," by which he means that there will never be an episode which self-consciously takes on an "issue." Much better, Whedon feels, is to seamlessly weave real issues into the plot, and Joss is a master at this. As has been often noted, the big conflicts on *Buffy* are issues that everyone can relate to. When Buffy's mom tells her she can't go out, it feels like the end of the world (of course, in her case, this is literally true). When Buffy becomes a teenage runaway, she winds up in hell (once again, literally). When Buffy gets a college roommate, she's a monster who's sucking the life out of her (you get the idea). Joss says that he knew he was doing something right when he talked with a female fan on a message board right after the first airing of "Innocence," in which Angel turns evil after sleeping with Buffy. "That's exactly what happened to me [after I slept with my boyfriend]," the fan told Joss.

Relentless Perfectionism

The sixth element of *Buffy*'s success is Joss's relentless perfectionism. Perfectionism is admirable in filmmaking; it's a recipe for heartache in television. With small budgets and only days to write and shoot each episode, television is the art of learning what's good enough. But there's no question, Joss is a perfectionist. Despite the pace and rigors of television, he's rarely given in to the urge to just get it done. He doesn't win every battle, but he does battle just the same. Parts of the very first *Buffy* episode, for example, were reshot eight months later so that Joss could improve certain scenes (as a midseason replacement, they had this luxury).

Despite the kudos for his writing, Joss is never satisfied. "I will say that I've been doing this for a while and I still think that every script I've written is the worst thing that I've ever done," says Whedon. "I think that is more of a writer thing than anything else. I don't know of any

"He was so answerful, so sweet . . ."
–Kimberly Hirsh, *www.jossisahottie.com*

Joss has countless Internet fans, but high on the list is Kimberly Hirsh, otherwise known as Kiba the Diva, and the force behind *www.jossisahottie.com*. I talked with her about her Joss site and, of course, Joss himself.

HAVENS: *What was it about Joss that made you want to develop a website dedicated to him?*

HIRSH: His capacity for kindly silliness. He took such an interest in his fans, and expressed himself in such a unique way . . . I watched *Buffy*, I chatted in the Bronze [the *Buffy* Internet discussion group], I liked the show. I even posted to Joss once for his thoughts on porn. He answered me! But I didn't begin to love Joss until I read other posts of his. He was so answerful, so sweet . . .

HAVENS: *Have you met him and what was that like?*

HIRSH: I've met Joss twice. Both times, it was exhilarating. I found myself giggling afterwards. Joss made me feel at ease, even amidst my fangirl excitement. It's so easy to converse with him. His conversation is quick-paced and witty, but not pretentious. He is considerate of his fans. And most importantly, he is real. He is a very real human, with both good points and flaws.

HAVENS: *Would you consider Joss to be as talented as someone like Steven Spielberg?*

HIRSH: I think Joss is a better storyteller than Spielberg. While his visuals aren't as striking, this may be because Spielberg usually has a significantly larger budget than Joss does. Where Spielberg typically strives for a happy ending, Joss never fears leaving his audience with an unsettling thought or image. Joss's work seems to have a deeper intertextuality to it, calling on ancient mythology and modern pop culture, all while telling a story about realistic people encountering situations which may seem fantastical but always are rooted in some emotional reality.

HAVENS: *What is it that you think makes Joss, well, Joss?*

HIRSH: What makes Joss Joss? Hmmm. Again, I can't emphasize his unique use of language enough. His understanding of human emotion. His awareness of the fact that his fans aren't rabid freaks, but rather people who truly admire his work.

good writer who is actually happy with something they've written. You are constantly worried about failing."

The perfectionist side of Joss is something his former professor understands. "I see it as a good thing," Professor Basinger says of Joss's excessive need to make things right. "I never thought of him as an obsessive personality, though. Joss is in many ways both very tense and very laid back. He was not someone at my door banging on it and screaming, 'What am I going to do next week?' But at the same time he wanted everything to be right. He wanted it to be the best he could make it. He didn't make his desire for the project to be the best it could be someone else's problem, ever. I think that is what bad perfectionists do. They punish all the rest of us. But Joss has never been like that.

"There's a story I tell that [exemplifies] that. Frank Capra, who was a good friend of mine, was here at Wesleyan to visit my comedy class. He was about eighty-three. I showed *Mr. Smith Goes to Washington,* and it was a beautiful day, and he strolled out on the campus while the film was running. When it got near the end, he came into the booth where I was to just see how it was going. He stood looking and was watching the big breakdown scene with Jimmy Stewart. By anybody's standards it is one of the greatest scenes in movie history. It's beautifully shot and cut. It's beautifully performed and written. All of a sudden, he gets upset and he runs outside, fuming. I ran after him and asked what was wrong. He said, 'I shouldn't have done it that way. It could have been better.'

"We are dealing with a rare breed when we are dealing with these guys. They are happy but there is always the sense that maybe I could have done it better. That's what makes them great. Yes, he'll be happy but not 100 percent."

Writing Comes First

The final, most important element to *Buffy*'s success is great writing. Much of this is generated by Joss himself, who, despite his many talents, still finds his greatest pleasure in sitting down and writing. One of Joss's most impressive assets is his ability to write quickly and well.

"We have so much to do that it doesn't really give you time for writer's block," says Whedon. "There are times when I sit and stare at a blank piece of paper for a few minutes but it doesn't last long. Most of the time I'm looking at things in arcs and I'm looking for what will move the story along and make the characters as interesting as possible."

"He is one of the busiest people I know," says *Buffy* executive producer Marti Noxon, "and he loves it. His brain just doesn't work like the rest of us mortals. He can write something in a few minutes that would take someone else a week to do, and it will be fantastic. We'll sit down for an hour meeting and you would be amazed by how much he can do during that time."

> His brain just doesn't work like the rest of us mortals.
> —Marti Noxon

It's clear that Joss is a brilliant writer, but no writer, however talented, can write twenty-two episodes a year. First and foremost, Joss had to attract and develop a team of talented writers. While he does a great deal on his own, Whedon is the first to admit that the shows are a collaborative effort. "I don't want it to sound like I don't listen to suggestions from the other writers, because I do. We have a great staff of creative people here who come up with some incredible ideas and they know these characters like their own family—probably better than their own families. We sit and talk about things during the hiatus and we work things out. When you are filming the shows, it's always too busy to take the time you need to really work out the details, so we do it in the spring and summer."

When he has the time, he powwows with the writers to better flesh out the stories for the upcoming year. Before the season begins, the main villains are set and the story arcs are decided. As the series progresses, the stories are written and Joss continues to keep his hand in every episode.

Whedon also knows the strengths of his writing and directing staff, which writer is best for a particular story and who should direct. There are certain writers who have the voice of a certain character down to a science. If that character is featured in a specific episode, then Joss tries to match them up to the best of his ability.

Joss has learned to leverage himself while inspiring his team. "When I get together with my writing team, I ask them, What is your favorite horror movie? What is the most embarrassing thing that ever happened to you? Now, how can we combine the two?"

Crucial to this organization is Joss's *Buffy* "Bible," which outlines the season. In season one, for example, Whedon had set the story arcs for the series and plotted the path for the main characters. At that point, he opened the creative process to other writers. The writing team, including Dana Reston, David Greenwalt, Rob Des Hotel, Dean Batali, Matt Kiene, and Joss Reinkemyer, had a plethora of stories to share. Joss soon knew they were all headed in the right direction. Whedon wrote the first two episodes of the season and then worked with this group of writers on the remaining ten.

"We all had ideas that seemed really scary," says Whedon, "but they wouldn't work until we could find the heart of the story. That part of my life was straight out of Dickens, who is one of my favorite writers. It was the best of times and it was the worst of times."

Balance between the various themes of the show can be difficult at times. "When you are working through that creative process, you can easily fall too heavy one way or another. It's a constant battle between the dark and the light," says Whedon. "We work hard to find a balance between the comedy, action, and horror of the show. And action and horror are actually more antithetical than comedy and horror, really, because horror is so much about not being in control of your environment. And in a way, comedy can be the same thing.

"Whereas with action–Buffy is a hero, she's somebody who really takes control of her environment. It's difficult to maintain that balance. But when it works, they really do mesh. Blood is kept to a minimum. The vampires disappear when you stake them and most of the monsters melt into the ground. It's a very environmentally conscious show," laughs the producer.

From the beginning, he wanted the audience to trust the core characters and that meant making sure each had a rich history from which to draw. "And what's fun about the show is, we never know from scene to scene which way it is going to go," Whedon tells. "A scene that starts out very dramatically could end up quite funny, or something truly horrible could happen in it. So it's not sort of, oh, here's the funny part, here's the scary part; we really never know what's going to be highlighted."

Whedon was more surprised than anyone that the WB let him get away with his style of storytelling. From the beginning, the network let Joss do what he felt was needed. There were a few arguments with Standards and Practices about certain jokes and some of the sexuality, but for the most part he was able to get away with, well, murder.

"We have had a long and good relationship with the network," says Whedon, "and they believed in what we were trying to do. We really couldn't have asked for more support in the beginning. This was a tough show to support and there really wasn't anything like it. Fox was doing the scary thing with *The X-Files*, but our show is more of a reach in a lot of ways. It wasn't easy to promote or market . . . It's an edgy show and unconventional.

"It's strange how all the pieces fall together for some shows and not others. I can't explain why, but sometimes it just works."

It certainly does work, and Whedon and his team have managed to integrate these seven elements to create a fan base whose size and enthusiasm haven't been matched since the early days of *Star Trek*.

Seven Seasons of Buffy

5

"My girlfriend's been dead for like six episodes and she keeps coming back. I don't think dying means a whole lot on this show. Maybe on ER."

—Adam Busch

For seven seasons, *Buffy the Vampire Slayer* has enthralled, delighted and infuriated fans. For all the variety of Joss Whedon's projects, the seven seasons of *Buffy* remain Joss' most influential and important body of work to date. This chapter explores, season by season, the process by which Joss developed his masterwork over the years. Focus is on the overall story arcs developed by Whedon and on the specific episodes that he wrote and directed.

Season one

As a midseason replacement show, *Buffy* was given the go ahead to create twelve episodes in the first season (as opposed to the usual 22 for a full season). Its renewal far from assured, Joss created a self-contained story arc twelve episodes long, beginning with Buffy's arrival in a new school and concluding with Buffy's final confrontation with the Master in episode twelve.

The opening two-parter, *Welcome to the Hellmouth* and *The Harvest*, was written by Whedon, who painstakingly oversaw every aspect of its production. Combined, these episodes make up almost ninety minutes of television and were an opportunity, in a sense, to remake the *Buffy* movie and do it right. Whedon, who had become accustomed to writing for big-budget movies, had to adjust to the limitations of his budget. On the *Buffy* season one DVD, Whedon talks the listener through the making of these first two episodes. What comes across most powerfully is Joss's continual realization that his big budget ideas would have to give way to the reality of his limited means.

But he didn't chafe under these restrictions; he almost seemed to welcome them. He quickly found that a small budget he could control was far better than an enormous budget that he couldn't. And Joss's focus on story and character made the budget limitations less important. He made the best of it, even declaring the small budget to be an asset to the show. "There's this thing called a budget you have to work and I think it makes you much more creative when you have a small one to work with. It forces you to concentrate on the story. I say this all the time but usually one or two vampires will work just as well as 100 if the story is good."

These two episodes embody almost everything Whedon was trying to accomplish with *Buffy*. These episodes succeed at what he calls his "genre-busting mission," successfully integrating horror, comedy, drama and action. He was determined to continually undermine convention and surprise the viewer. He began the series with the classic scene of a vampire luring an innocent blond to her doom, only to have the viewer realize that the blond (Darla) is the vampire!

The core of the show was built around the four main characters. While Buffy is the main character, the three other leads in season one are strong, nuanced characters. Giles, the stuffy watcher, is brave, loving and with a mysterious past of his own. Willow is her geeky best friend who grows increasingly less geeky and more powerful over the course of the series. Xander (Nicholas Brendan) is equally complex, equal parts brave and buffoonish, wise and foolish.

Jesse, Xander's best friend, is introduced as one of the original gang. When the vampires attack, Jesse is captured and held hostage as bait for the others. This is the normal convention in television action shows. The main characters can't die, so the villains find some excuse not to kill them (this sort of thing drives Joss crazy; "kill them already" he cries). But Joss was just pretending; the vampires have killed Jesse (they've made him into a vampire) and ultimately Xander will have to stake, if accidentally, his best friend. Joss wanted to include Jesse in the opening credits to increase the shock factor, but he didn't have the budget to

ALBERT L. ORTEGA

The season one *Buffy* cast, from the days when all they had to worry about were vampires and bug ladies.

produce two opening scenes.

The next nine episodes, while continuing the story arc launched in the two-parter, were designed as self-contained episodes. Each presented a stand-alone plot, complete with its own villain and tidy resolution at the conclusion. Buffy fought and defeated witches, demon robots, bug ladies, hyena spirits and invisible girls. The first season, while not always holding to the quality level of the pilot episodes, was strong and began to build enthusiasm among both critics and fans.

Joss didn't direct any of these first eleven episodes. He probably would have liked to but his miserable experience creating the pilot convinced him he still had a lot to learn. And he was determined to learn it, despite the fact that Hollywood doesn't particularly support writers who aspire to direct. "Part of the reason I made the TV show *Buffy* is because as a writer—even a successful one—in Hollywood, when you say you want to direct movies, they're appalled. They look like, 'Do you kill babies?' I mean, they're just shocked. 'What? You want to what?' 'I'm a storyteller. I want to tell stories. I want to direct.' 'Uh, I don't get it. You want to what?' And people actually said to me, 'Well, if you'd directed a video.' I'm like, just once, somebody please say to a video director, 'Well, if you'd written a script. If you just knew how to tell a story.' Not that all writers can direct, or should, or want

> when you say you want to direct movies, they're appalled. They look like, 'Do you kill babies?' —Joss

to. I'm sure a lot of writers want to direct because they're bitter, which is not a reason to direct. I want to speak visually, and writing is just a way of communicating visually. That's what it's all about. But nobody would even consider me to direct. So I said, 'I'll create a television show, and I'll use it as a film school, and I'll teach myself to direct on TV.'"

By episode twelve Joss was ready and he wrote and directed *Prophecy Girl*, the season one finale. From this point on Joss would direct every episode he wrote (excepting a few episodes he co-wrote with David Greenwalt). *Prophecy Girl* was an important episode for the new program. The first eleven episodes were, as a whole, excellent television. But *Prophecy Girl* was a masterpiece, wonderfully written and tightly constructed. It's easy to forget how much Whedon packed into this 40-odd minutes of television: the resolution of Xander's season long infatuation with Buffy, the elevating of Willow to a new level of pathos after she discovers the student corpses, the shifting of Cordelia from bitch-goddess to semi-Scooby, and, of course, Buffy's death and the defeat of the Master.

But *Prophecy Girl* is most notable for the emotional intensity of the script and of Sarah Michelle Gellar's Buffy. After eleven episodes of heroism, defeating witches and bug ladies, demon robots and invisible girls, Joss took Buffy to a new place. He created a situation in which Buffy, genuinely courageous, is overwhelmed with fear. This is a place few action writers have gone. Can you imagine Batman hysterical with fear? But Whedon did this quite deliberately, because he wanted the audience to remember that Buffy is a sixteen-year-old girl who happens to have superpowers, not a superhero that happens to reside in a sixteen-year-old girl. We admire Superman and enjoy the action, but our hearts don't break over him, and we can't relate to him.

The critical scene is Buffy's confrontation with Giles and Angel after she discovers that the prophecy guarantees her death in the confrontation with the Master:

> BUFFY: So that's it, huh? I remember the drill. One Slayer dies, next one's called! Wonder who she is. (to Giles) Will you train her? Or will they send someone else?
>
> GILES: Buffy, I . . .
>
> BUFFY: They say how he's gonna kill me? Do you think it'll hurt? *Tears are flowing freely from her eyes. Angel tries to hug her, but she puts up her hands and quickly steps away.*
>
> BUFFY: Don't touch me! (to Giles) Were you even gonna tell me?
>
> GILES: I was hoping that I wouldn't have to. That there was . . . some way around it. I . . .
>
> BUFFY: I've got a way around it. I quit!
>
> ANGEL: It's not that simple.
>
> BUFFY: I'm making it that simple! I quit! I resign, I'm fired, you can find someone else to stop the Master from taking over!
>
> GILES: I'm not sure that anyone else can. All the signs indicate . . .
>
> BUFFY: The signs? (throws a book at him) Read me the signs! (throws another one) Tell me my fortune! You're so useful sitting here with all your books. You're really a lotta help!
>
> GILES: No, I don't suppose I am.
>
> ANGEL: I know this is hard.
>
> BUFFY: What do you know about this? You're never gonna die!
>
> ANGEL: You think I want anything to happen to you? Do you think I could stand it? We just gotta figure out a way. . .
>
> BUFFY: I already did. I quit, remember? Pay attention!
>
> GILES: Buffy, if the Master rises . . .
>
> BUFFY: (yanks the cross from her neck) I don't care! (calms down) I don't care. Giles, I'm sixteen years old. I don't wanna die.

In this scene Gellar first demonstrated a powerful emotional intensity which would become a core strength of the series, particularly in season two.

Professor Basinger, talking about *Prophecy Girl*, relates, "I remember a moment, I think it was the first season where Buffy is in her prom dress with a leather jacket. She rises up and starts to walk with her crossbow down into the bowels of the earth to confront the evil. There's

something about it. Whenever someone asks, 'Why is *Buffy* great?' that comes to my mind. There is something so elegant, noble, mythic and astonishing that you are watching your TV set and you are seeing this. This is a high school girl, but she's like a warrior woman. It's funny that she's in her prom dress at the same time it is masterfully frightening. That's Joss."

In *Prophecy Girl*, Whedon demonstrated that, despite his origins as a writer, he makes a credible director, a demonstration that would become more impressive as the series wore on. Whedon would later go on to allow a number of his writers to direct, including Marti Noxon, Douglas Petrie and David Fury, further validating his view that excellent writers often have what it takes to become excellent directors.

> This is a high school girl, but she's like a warrior woman. It's funny that she's in her prom dress at the same time it is masterfully frightening. That's Joss.
> —Professor Basinger

Season two

In season two *Buffy* cemented its place in the hearts of both fans and critics. Whedon had hit his stride and the series succeeded at every level—wonderful comedy, genuine horror, fantastic action and, most of all, awesomely intense drama. Joss was fully immersed in the show, carefully reviewing every script and every scene. He wrote and directed five episodes in season two and co-wrote one as well.

In season two Whedon expanded and deepened the importance of the story arc. Unlike in season one, many season two episodes are fully devoted to the on-going story arc and character evolution. This shift played to the strengths of the series.

Joss wrote and directed the first episode of the season, *When She Was Bad*. This episode was a wonderful follow-up on *Prophecy Girl*. Joss again broke convention by showing the dark side of Buffy, which, as it emerges, is a reaction to the intensity of fear she experienced in facing the Master. This episode, in showing a victory that has consequences and a superhero with scars, is part of Whedon's on-going efforts to remind the viewer that Buffy remains human and vulnerable, however strong she may be.

Season two introduces Spike, a vampire villain, and Oz, a character

Sarah Michelle Gellar and Charisma Carpenter.
Who gets your vote for homecoming queen?

Alyson Hannigan (Willow)

One of Joss' most critical insights in creating *Buffy* was his portrayal of Willow. It would have been easy to make Willow the mousy, brainy sidekick so frequently seen on TV and in the movies. But Joss' Willow is as complex a character as Buffy—meek but courageous, smart but sensitive, intensely vulnerable but surprisingly tough. The role of Willow has turned out to be central to the series and it's hard to imagine a better Willow than Alyson Hannigan. No character on Buffy has evolved as much as Willow, but Hannigan manages each transition—from shy virgin to werewolf-dating Wicca to lesbian addict to 'evil Willow'—with aplomb.

SUE SCHNEIDER / MOONGLOW PHOTOS

"There was a certain innocent strength about Alyson that came through when she was reading for the part," Whedon says. "She seemed confident one minute and the next she was so vulnerable. Of course it took us a while to see how good she would be in the role. Much like Sarah we put Alyson through hell. The network had their pick and we had ours and it was a big push and pull kind of thing."

"I seriously thought there was no way I was going to get the role. We auditioned and

Alyson Hannigan hangs out with boyfriend Alexis Denisof.

auditioned," says Hannigan. "It got down to just a few of us and I didn't think I had a prayer."

A few weeks later she got the call that she had won the role.

"I know everyone says this, but I really was shocked," Hannigan laughs. "I couldn't wait to start work. I was just so excited."

From the beginning Hannigan felt a kinship with the Willow character. "In some of those early shows Willow is afraid to speak out and I know just how she feels," says Hannigan. "I'm better now, but there were times in my life when I just couldn't speak because I was so afraid. Do I understand that whole not fitting into high school thing? Yes!"

"We, Willow and I, have a great deal in common. I'm incredibly shy and worry about what others might think. That is so much of what Willow was about in those early days. I like that she was smart and sort of bookish. She's also had a chance to experience life in a way that most people don't, and as an actress I've had that same thing. So there's a lot of me in her and vice versa."

There's something else the character and actress share. "You aren't expecting anything and then all off the sudden Ally says something that makes you bend over laughing," says Brendon. "Let's just say for such a sweet woman she can say some pretty wild stuff."

> Let's just say for such a sweet woman she can say some pretty wild stuff.
> —Nicholas Brendon

Like Gellar, Hannigan has been in the acting business since she was a toddler, when she began doing commercials for Oreos and McDonalds. When the Washington D.C. native was 11, her family moved from Atlanta to Los Angeles where she appeared in the films *My Stepmother is an Alien* and on the television shows *Almost Home*, *The Torkelsons* and *George*. On *Buffy* Hannigan has made the best of the skills she'd honed in her early acting career, and over the seasons she enlarged her character into a complex, multi-faceted individual. As a result, fans have watched Willow evolve from a mousy doormat to sexy powerful Wiccan.

"You know I've grown up too," laughs Hannigan. "I used to worry all the time that I'd do or say the wrong thing. I was always putting my foot in my mouth. Now I'm used to the taste of feet. And, like my character, I'm a lot better about speaking my mind."

Joss having fun with Alyson Hannigan and Seth Green.

Whedon based on someone he knew. "I just knew a guy named Oz. Kinda short. Played lead guitar for a band. He had this incredible cool about him; he wore bowling shirts before anybody else did." Fans were initially cool to Oz, but ultimately he became a very important part of the series.

One of Joss' favorite episodes, and certainly one of the greatest episodes of the series, is *Innocence*, which Joss wrote and directed. This is the episode where Angel becomes Angelus as a result of the consummation of his relationship with Buffy. *Innocence* was notable in any number of ways, including featuring the first sex scenes between Buffy and Angel.

These were the first sex scenes Joss had ever directed and he was embarrassed. "I felt very awkward. The actors, however, both extraordinary pros and good friends, were fine. They were laughing and scratching, and just sort of, you know, put my hand where and do what and what do you need? I think they were sort of amused by how embarrassed I was."

Perhaps the most powerful scene in *Innocence* is the first confrontation between Buffy and Angel after he loses his soul. It's a scene of great emotional power and exquisite cruelty. Initially filmed outside, Whedon quickly realized that the scene should take place in the bedroom. The result is brilliant and the episode shows how much Whedon had grown as both a writer and director.

In *Innocence* Angel turns bad, and a few episodes later, in *Passion*, we see just how bad. In this episode Angelus ruthlessly hunts down and kills Jenny Calendar. The scene is brutal and it's classic Joss. On one level, it's a riveting scene, truly horrific. On another level it accomplishes a larger objective; it shows that Angel is truly evil, "not pretending, not a little bad." It also served as a warning to the cast—be good because everyone is expendable.

> I think they were sort of amused by how embarrassed I was.
> —Joss

"It keeps you on your toes," says James Marsters. "You never know what might happen next, so you damn well better come in here and be a professional about the whole thing. If they don't like you, and a lot of times even if they do, you could wind up gone."

The two-part season finale, *Becoming*, was written and directed by Whedon. These episodes accomplish the seemingly impossible task of pushing up the emotional intensity yet another notch. Joss plays the Willow card again, putting her in mortal peril and, interestingly, giving the audience a hint of the power she would some day possess. All the stops are pulled out as Buffy's support network is taken away one piece at a time; as she lost Angel, she now loses her place in school and her home. Ultimately, she is forced to kill Angel, no longer evil and

> If they don't like you, and a lot of times even if they do, you could wind up gone.
> —James Marsters

very much the love of her life, in order to save the world. The episodes conclude with Buffy, looking like nothing so much as another runaway teenager, getting on a bus out of town. It's a heartbreaking ending.

Season three

By season three *Buffy* was running smoothly and Whedon, while still involved in every aspect of production, could emerge from the details, knowing that his team would do things the way he wanted them. Joss

Nicholas Brendon (Xander)

As one of the original cast members, Brendon has fought by Buffy's side since the beginning. Brendon has a great deal in common with his character. They are both nice guys with a quick dry wit. And they are both incredibly silly at times.

It's easy to see the common theme that drew the *Buffy* cast together. Like Joss, Sarah and Alyson, Brendon (who stuttered and was painfully shy) had a horrible time in high school. "I think sometimes that the shy people become actors because it gives us a chance to express ourselves in ways we never imagined," Brendon says. "In high school I could have never imagined getting to be a part of something like this."

Brendon's early aspirations were to be a professional athlete, but he was sidetracked after an injury and began studying acting. With the help of a speech pathologist he was able to lose the stutter and life began to improve. Before joining *Buffy*, Brendon worked a variety of jobs including being a plumber's assistant and script delivery boy.

"There were times in the beginning where I seriously wondered if I was ever going to make enough money to eat being an actor, but it was just something I had to do. Getting a role like this on such a great show doesn't happen to many people and I know how damn lucky I am," says the actor.

While his resume has a quite a few credits listed, *Buffy* was his first significant acting job. When he won the role, the Los Angeles native was working as a waiter and it was a tough time financially. Then this magical role appeared and he knew he had to do whatever it took to get it.

> He's the guy. We all know that guy from high school; some of us were him. —Joss

"Joss created this guy we could all relate to in some way. For the most part he was invisible to everyone except Buffy and Willow. That's why, years after high school, he is still so devoted to them both. They cared about him when no one else did."

"What am I going to say about him," says Whedon of Xander. "He's the guy. We all know that guy from high school; some of us were him. Then he grows up and he isn't sure what he wants to be. As he matures he realizes what it is he doesn't want to be. The thing about this character is

Nicholas Brendon answers questions for fans.

loyalty. He sticks with his friends, many times to the detriment of his relationships with other people."

As for comparisons between himself and the character he plays, Brendon believes there are quite a few. "In some ways I'm just like him and in others we have nothing in common," says Brendon. "We've both grown and matured through the years. He still has a lot of problems with his relationships, and thankfully I've grown past a lot of that. He's seen what his parents have become. Sort of his own demons, and now he's afraid of the whole settling down thing.

"I on the other hand am loving married life."

Oh and about that dance thing Xander does. Was that something the writers created for him or did he make it up himself?

"Yes, um, well that's me. I was doing these crazy dances all the time and they just sort of wrote it into the show. Hey, whatever it takes for the laugh, right?"

again wrote and directed five episodes and began planning an *Angel* spin-off that would launch in *Buffy's* fourth season.

Season three introduced some wonderful plot developments—Willow and Xander's budding romance, the fastidious mayor and his henchmen, the introduction of Faith and her descent into evil, and Buffy's flirtation with the dark side of slayerdom. While matching the intensity of season two was a challenge, season three comes close, with perhaps the biggest contribution made by Eliza Dushku as the electrifying but troubled new slayer.

Joss opened season three with Buffy as a runaway waitress in Los Angeles. In *Anne*, which Joss wrote and directed, Buffy again faces the conflict between her desire to flee her responsibilities and her deep sense of duty. Again *Buffy* presents a real-life theme in fantasy guise. A runaway flees her family problems only to find life on the streets a living hell. Of course in *Buffy*, the hell is real.

Buffy returns to Sunnydale and reconciles with her friends and family. Angel returns, first in an animal-like mental state, but soon regaining his wits and sanity. It's typical of Joss that he doesn't simply return Angel to the relatively cuddly good vampire role he plays in season one and early season two. The audience has seen too much and Angel has gone too far to be easily forgiven. How can the audience ever embrace Angel again after what he has done? In *Amends* Joss wrote and directed an episode designed specifically to address this problem. Angel is tormented by voices driving him towards evil and he is losing the power to resist. Rather than yield, he chooses suicide. The guilt and pain are too much for him. In a scene of incredible intensity Buffy begs him to continue fighting. In the ambiguous ending, it seems Angel's life is saved through divine intervention. Angel's suffering wins a place for him back in our hearts. Equally importantly, Angel finds his purpose—to make amends for his past—and here Joss is also helping to set up for the *Angel* spinoff.

For sheer fun, it's hard to beat *Doppelgangland* (also written and directed by Joss). In this episode, Joss stepped back from the intensity of his last few scripts to deliver some unadulterated fun. Having spotted a good thing in the alternative universe's vampire Willow from the episode *Wish*, he found an (admittedly feeble) excuse to bring her to Sunnydale. This episode previews a darker side of Willow that would emerge in season six. It also foreshadows Willow's lesbianism, which would emerge in season four.

The second half of season three focuses on Faith's decent into evil. Faith shifts from a troubled slayer to a human monster as scary as any latex creation. But as scary as Faith becomes she remains fully human, and her relationship with the Mayor is truly touching. "One of my favorite moments," Whedon relates, "was when Harry Groener who was playing the mayor asked me if he was supposed to care about Faith or if he was just using her. I had not considered that question before and it led to a very beautiful, completely twisted father-daughter relationship that I thought was one of the loveliest things we did on the show. I knew where they were going as to who was going to live and who was going to die, but I didn't know that [the Mayor and Faith would have a loving relationship]. Having the space to find that as you go is what makes a season a wonderful thing to create."

SUE SCHNEIDER / MOONGLOW PHOTOS

The elctrifying Eliza Dushku. Faith is back for a number of episodes in *Buffy's* season seven, and there has been speculation that she could permanently join the series if Gellar leaves after the season's end. *Faith the Vampire Slayer*?

Despite Whedon's unassuming style, there was no question that he was fully in charge of every aspect of the series. Unlike some productions, which seemed to be run by committee, there was no conflicting authority or confused decision making on *Buffy*—Joss was the boss. At the same time Joss remained receptive to his production team and actors. For example, Joss was receptive when Gellar struggled with the direction the plot was taking in season three. Faith was clearly moving toward the dark side and, to Gellar's thinking, Buffy should have picked up Faith's duplicity.

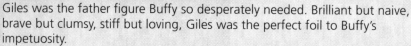

Giles was the father figure Buffy so desperately needed. Brilliant but naive, brave but clumsy, stiff but loving, Giles was the perfect foil to Buffy's impetuosity.

"I've always seen him as the trustworthy sort and a very calm person," says Head. "There were times through the years when he certainly lost his temper, but for the most part he was the calming force of the group. He began as this sort of bookish librarian who had a great deal of knowledge about vampires and monsters but had never run across them. He knew nothing of real life.

"At the same time, we know that he has a rather disreputable past and is more or less atoning for his sins by helping the slayer. There was a time when he was quite the wild man."

Before *Buffy,* most Americans knew Head, if at all, from his romantic Taster's Choice commercials. But Head's been a successful actor for years. Born in Camden Town, England, in 1954, Head began acting on stage and was in productions of *The Rocky Horror Picture Show, Julius Caesar, The Heiress, Chess, Yonasab,* and *Rope.* In 1977, he took on a series of guest roles on British television. The actor's first full-time acting job was on the series *Enemy at the Door.* He went on to do several more series and starred in the films *Lady Chatterley's Lover, A Prayer for the Dying,* and *Devil's Hill.*

Head was a series regular on the short-lived Fox series *VR.5,* and made several guest appearances on *Highlander: The Series, NYPD Blue,* and *Spenser for Hire.*

When the role of Rupert Giles came along, he wasn't sure what to think. Like many of his younger costars, Head was as surprised as anyone when *Buffy* took off. "I've worked for many years, and it is difficult to know in advance what will be a success," says Head. "I knew we were working with a superb script and had a talented cast, but it is very much up to the audience to decide what will be a success."

Over the years, Head's stalwart Giles stood by his slayer and helped her through the more difficult times. He's been punched, kicked, and whacked unconscious countless times, but he says it's all a part of the job.

"In no way has my role on the show been as physical as Sarah's, but there have been moments. There were times when I had to do certain things that meant being in good shape, but I've survived," says Head.

Fans were heartbroken when Giles left Buffy behind to return home to England. Head is still a recurring character, but he felt he had to step down and go back and live with his family in England.

"The man has been away from home for more than six years and it was time for him to go back," says Whedon. "Changes get made. The show evolves. It is a big hole. Anthony will be on the show on a recurring basis. We'll be bringing him back a lot, because we love him. He left us when the kids were entering the grownup world. And, of course, they handle it just as badly as possible. But they don't really need or don't really know how to relate to a mentor figure. He was the grownup on the show. They're now sort of becoming grownups.

"At first I didn't want him to step down, I didn't want that void. But in a way it sort of works for the show. Buffy doesn't need somebody to tell her what to do now. She needs to figure it out on her own. So now I want to feel that lack, because they're going to feel it. They're constantly going to be going 'If Giles were here somebody else could explain this,' or 'we'd have a grown-up who knew what to do and we're still new at this.' And I want the audience to feel the same way the characters do; that's always the mandate on the show. So no, we won't be bringing in another watcher."

Originally he left to spend more time with his family and to do the *Buffy* spin-off, *Ripper*. Unfortunately, Joss's busy schedule with his new series, *Firefly*, has put *Ripper* on hold temporarily. Instead, Head has been busy working on a new series, *Manchild*.

SUE SCHNEIDER / MOONGLOW PHOTOS

A dapper-looking Anthony Head.

"It's something that we definitely want to do and there's great interest in the story," says Whedon of *Ripper*. "The timing is just sort of bad right now."

Head will do ten shows out of twenty-two in season seven. "He's like that family member who lives far away, and you only get to see him every once in a while," Whedon says, "and that's what makes it special."

For Head, working on the series was a blessing. "I've worked on so many shows where there were too many different people trying to control what was happening, and it was a complete mess. We don't have that with *Buffy*. Joss knows how every single thing that is involved with the show must go, and the rest of us follow his lead. He's made a terribly appealing show that is enjoyed by people of all ages, and that's quite an amazing task when you think about it," Head declares.

Whedon is clearly delighted with Head's contribution. "Tony is great. A real actor. He really cares about the craft. It's all there. The only conflict Tony and I have is that I always want him to give me less. He always wants to get out there and put it all on screen. I keep going, 'The British guy–more restrained!'"

Joss and some of the season four cast, with Alyson Hannigan and Emma Caulfield looking mischievous.

"There was one point several seasons ago when I turned to Joss and said, 'I'm not happy,'" says Gellar. "I just don't feel like myself. I feel like Buffy's being pushed around by everybody. By Faith, by this one, she's not trusting anybody, and I really feel like she's lost herself and I'm unhappy because I can't figure out why I'm doing these things.

"And we sat down and we talked, and he said, 'you know what? I see what you're talking about.'

"Do you have any idea what it feels like as an actor when the creator of your show will sit down and talk with you like that? And to know that you can trust him to fix whatever problem it is. There are times when I've gone to him and I didn't understand why we were doing certain things and he explains it in such a way that it all makes sense. You just have to trust in that genius," says Gellar.

You just have to trust in that genius.
—Sarah Michelle Gellar

The end of season three marks the Scoobies' graduation from high school and, predictably, they depart with a bang. Again writing and directing the two-part season finale, Joss created a giant CGI snake, blew up the school and brought the high school class together amid a hail of flaming arrows ("because you have to have flaming arrows" he says). Evil is vanquished, Buffy graduates, and Angel heads off to L.A. and his own series.

Season four

Season four takes the Scoobies out of high school and into the world of college and work. Buffy finds new love, defeats a demon/human cyborg and takes on a secret paramilitary initiative.

Joss was equally busy. Even while overseeing the launch of *Angel* he continued to look for new ways to challenge himself as a writer and a director. The result was *Hush*, an episode in which most of the episode— 29 minutes—was without any spoken dialogue. What could have been a gimmick show became a memorable, horrifying episode.

Hush is one of Joss' favorites and it's no accident that it was nominated for an Emmy. It is one of *Buffy's* best conceived and most celebrated episodes. "I like being able to experiment when I write," says Joss, "and 'Hush' is exactly that. If it challenges and makes me think in a different way, then it's a lot more fun."

"He called me to talk about 'Hush,'" says Professor Jeanine Basinger. "He asked what films there were about someone who couldn't speak and I suggested the *Spiral Staircase*. She's a mute and knows who the murderer is, and he's trying to kill her. And of course she can't tell anybody. He doesn't really need this in any way. He just likes a sounding board. He always comes up with his own original idea. He'll call me for what movies he should be looking at for certain ideas, and it's very flattering for me that he cares to ask."

Season four also introduces a romance between Willow and Tara. Fans were shocked when they realized where the relationship was heading, but for Joss it was a natural progression.

> I like love stories, and that's what [the] Willow and Tara story is. —Joss

"I like love stories," says Joss, "and that's what [the] Willow and Tara story is. We've seen Willow grow and mature in these other relationships and then when Tara came along, it just made sense. In college, well, that's where most people begin to explore their sexuality. We put Willow and Tara into situations, as witches, that were somewhat physical but not sexual. And as their relationship began to mature we saw them together in a different way. At the time the network was more than a little wary about having a gay couple on the show. They didn't want anything too intimate and there was to be no kissing involved. But as the story moved along, so did the network. The fans have embraced the story in a way even I couldn't have imagined, and it's meant a great deal to a lot of people out there."

The lesbian story line was a surprise to Hannigan, but one she was more than willing to take on. "I know it upset some of the fans, but the truth is I've been so grateful to have been able to touch so many lives with this story. People walk up to me to this day and tell me thank you for bringing such a wonderful love story to life. I tell them it was the writers and Joss who are to thank. They did it and they did it in a respectful and loving way."

The network was nervous about the onscreen romance, but Joss had a strategy for managing this. "We got away with it because we didn't tell them what we were doing."

There was some fan discontent in season four, over specific issues (like Willow and Tara), but mostly regarding the quality of the season. This discontent was misguided; while not all of the ambitions in season four were realized, the overall quality was strong. At the same time, it appeared that Joss was taking on too much.

"I really have no idea [how I will juggle two shows]," Joss admitted. "I am burned out already. [*Angel* executive producer] David Greenwalt and I just stare at each other balefully and say, 'What were we thinking?' I think my life is over, and that's just something I have to deal with. [Seriously], I don't know how it's done. Basically, it just means I work harder. We were working 16 hours a day on *Buffy*, and now we work 16 hours a day, but more concentrated. It's more mentally exhausting. But it's not like you can let it slide. I still don't work on Sundays when I can avoid it. Now I'm actually firm about not working Sundays, since I'm so burned out after the week, more so than before."

Joss wrote and directed the season four finale, *Restless*. Interestingly, Joss had resolved the main conflict (destroying the cyborg Adam) in the previous episode. The final episode is an extended dream sequence, featuring dreams by each of the four main characters as their sleep is invaded by the spirit of the first slayer.

This innovative episode creates a spooky and surreal David Lynch ambience and, like *Hush*, pushed Whedon as a writer and director. It covers a lot of territory, including a highly erotic scene of Willow body painting Tara, a battle with the first slayer and Armin Shimerman (the actor who played the Principal through season three) as Walter Kurtz from *Apocalypse Now*. Every scene is soaked with subtle meanings, references and foreshadowing. Except, Joss hastens to add, the cheese-man. "People never believe me when I say the cheese-man meant NOTHING," Joss reveals. "Cheese makes me laugh."

Season five

Like every season before it, season five takes *Buffy* in a new direction, with a new set of issues and characters. The first episode ends with the enigmatic introduction of Dawn, Buffy's mysterious younger sister. The story centers around Glory, an immensely powerful Goddess bent on the destruction of Dawn, the opening of a portal to a hell dimension, and, in the process, the destruction of Earth as we know it. Season five is wonderfully done and raises a set of core issues, including friendship, grief, death, sisterhood and independence. It also shot down criticism that Joss was spread too thin to maintain *Buffy's* quality.

The first episode, a funny and enthralling encounter between Buffy and Dracula, is on its surface a stand-alone episode. But *Buffy vs. Dracula* cleverly sets up the story arc for the season. This episode highlights the insecurities that ultimately lead to Riley's departure. It also, in Xander's determination to stop being "everybody's butt-monkey," showed us the motivation that would ultimately lead to Xander's emergence from the basement and his engagement to Anya. And most importantly, the episode introduces Dawn, who would become a regular on the program.

Michelle Trachtenberg won the coveted role of Buffy's younger sister. Trachtenberg knew she was joining a successful show and was already a big fan when she came on board. Like Gellar and Hannigan, the young Trachtenberg was already a Hollywood veteran, having begun acting at the age of four. She played Lily Montgomery on *All My Children*, was a series regular on *The Adventures of Pete & Pete* and made several guest appearances on *Meego*, *Guys Like Us*, *Figure it Out*, *Dave's World*, *Law & Order* and *Clarissa Explains it All*. She'd starred in the feature films *Harriet the Spy*, *Inspector Gadget*, *Can't Be Heaven*, *The Cage* and *Melissa*.

And she did all of this before turning 16.

Getting the role as Buffy's little sister was one of the best moments of Trachtenberg's career. "I was so happy, because I was such a big fan of the show already," laughs the actress. "I couldn't believe that I was actually going to get to hang out with these cool people and characters every day."

Trachtenberg fit right in with the *Buffy* cast; it didn't hurt that she already knew Gellar. "She had worked on *All My Children* and I knew her from there. She has become like a real sister to me, and in the beginning, she and everyone else was worried about how I was doing. Was I happy? Was everything going OK? They make you feel very loved and a part of the family," says Trachtenberg.

When she joined the show the character Dawn was called the Key. In the beginning, Trachtenberg wasn't clear on what that meant. She says Joss told her in an early meeting that Dawn was a regular teen who was a Key, and even he didn't know how it was going to all work out.

"I'm not sure if he didn't know, or if he really didn't want to put too much on me at once, but it worked," says the actress. "We've really developed—I almost feel like I've been a part of the show from the beginning because I've been watching it since its debut and I'm a little walking *Buffy* encyclopedia, rather scary but it's fine."

> I'm a little walking *Buffy* encyclopedia, rather scary but it's fine.
> —Michelle Trachtenberg

In the touching episode *Family*, which Whedon wrote and directed, Joss did for Tara what he did for Oz in *Innocence*—he made us love her. Some fans were having difficulty accepting Tara as part of the Scooby gang. In typical Joss fashion, he took this head on, painting Tara as even more of an outsider as the Scoobies struggle with what to give her for her birthday. But conflict with Tara's family forces the Scoobies to choose sides. They ultimately choose Tara as their own and, more importantly, we desperately want them to make this choice.

Even more important, in *Family*, Joss returned to one of *Buffy's* "mission statements." Your family can be difficult and cruel, Joss tells us, but you have the power to create your own family. Your new family can be more important, more real, than the family you are born into. This theme replays itself throughout the series, from the initial formation of the

Scoobies in season one to Xander's failed attempt to form a new family with Anya in season six.

As Joss tells it: "When we created the show, they said, 'Do you want [Buffy's] family?' And I said, 'Well, mom and whatnot, but basically, she has a family. Her father is Giles, her sister is Willow, and it's already in place.' I had some things go on in my life that made me say, 'I really want to get this message out, that it's not about blood.' Tara was the perfect vehicle for that.

"*Family* is as much of a didactic message show as I've ever done. Hopefully an entertaining one." This theme is obviously heartfelt for Joss, but he insists it's no reflection on his up-

Michelle Trachtenberg poses with Sarah Michelle Gellar.

bringing. "I actually love my family!" he laughs. "We've been an unconventional family. I was a child of divorce, and there was a lot of shuffling around. And [there were] people who were not in my family who became of my family."

A particularly innovative episode was *The Body*, which was later nominated for an Emmy. The episode, written and directed by Whedon, employs long scenes with minimal cuts to convey a deeper sense of physicality and reality. Joss had lost his mother a few years before and the episode had a special poignancy for him.

> I really want to get this message out, that it's not about blood.
> —Joss

"I really made the episode to capture something very small. The black ashes in your mouth numbness of death. The very morbid physicality of it. It's why Buffy threw up. Why Dawn said she had to pee. Why the girls kissed. Why there were so many shots of the body.

"You know, I worked my ass off on [that episode]. And my whole cast was extraordinary. But I really thought people were going to sort of hate it, because the whole point was, there's no catharsis. There's no point where you go, 'We've learned this!' or 'She'll always be a part of us!' It was just, 'My mother is a dead body. And that's all.' But people actually did get a kind of catharsis from it. A lot of people who have lost people said it really helped them deal with it or it really moved them. I was surprised by that, because my intention was just to capture that reality, not really to comment on it or be helpful about it.

"The reactions of all the characters were based on things I've done. My mother was not the first person I lost. The first person I ever lost, there was a whole thing where I had to find a black tie, because I thought you had to wear a black tie to a funeral. Of course, it was California, so people showed up in Hawaiian shirts, but I didn't know that! And I couldn't find one anywhere in LA. I went to dozens of stores, and I was sweating and shaking, like, 'If I don't find this, it'll be sacrilege!' That's where the Willow thing came from.

"And then when I lost my mother, there was that numbness that I tried to capture with *Buffy*, but at the same time, I had already lost someone, and I was around a lot of people who hadn't so then I was sort of in Tara's shoes—watching other people's reactions, and just trying to help and get through it. So it's all there. Everybody's got a piece of that."

The finale of season five, *The Gift*, represented the culmination of a story arc that Whedon had forshadowed in season three. As everyone knows, Buffy sacrificed herself to save the world—the ultimate sacrifice. Or was it?

By the end of season five Whedon portrayed a Buffy that is traumatized and deeply tired. She has lost Angel, Riley and her mother and the resolution she showed when she killed Angel at the end of season two has faded. She isn't willing to kill Dawn, whatever the consequences. When she realizes that she can die in Dawn's place, her reaction is... relief. "The hardest thing to do in this world is to live in it."

So Joss kills Buffy in a brilliant episode that broke fans' hearts. "Our mandate was: MAKE THEM CRY! And when we watched it, we all cried," says Joss. But not everyone was thrilled with this development, including some of his cast.

"I went straight to Joss," Marsters says. "I said, 'Joss, you can't kill Buffy. The show is called *Buffy the Vampire Slayer*! You can't do that, man—I need the job!'

"Joss looked me straight in the eye and said, 'Dude, it's my show. I can do whatever I want.'

"He smiled his little trickster smile and left," the actor recalls, "which led me to believe that I'd have my job, not to worry. And I think this was the most dramatic way to close the original thesis of the show, which was, 'How does one get from childhood to adulthood? How does one pass through adolescence?'

> Joss looked me straight in the eye and said, 'Dude, it's my show. I can do whatever I want.'
> —James Marsters

"Now the question for Buffy and the Scooby Gang is, 'How does one negotiate the perils of adulthood?' And a bloody good corollary is, 'What's Spike's role in that process?'"

Buffy's death was equally stressful for executives at UPN, who had picked up the series from the WB.

The Move to UPN

There are times when the WB made suggestions that didn't sit well with Whedon, but for the most part they gave him free reign. From its beginnings as a mid-season replacement, *Buffy* had evolved into a very important show for the WB, a show that helped define the network. And in return Whedon received creative freedom and, almost as important, respect for his creation.

But things turned rocky as WB's five-year contract for *Buffy* approached its end. Fox, which spent $2 million per episode producing *Buffy* but only received $1 million per episode from the WB, expected a large increase in its fee. This was normal for the television business. Production companies typically sold their shows for less than production costs, making up the difference with international and syndication sales for their hits. And with large increases in fees at the five year renewal point.

While this was typical for the television business, it wasn't typical for the WB, which as a fairly new network was losing $50 million per year and had never before had a show reach the five-year mark. In the negotiation process, Jamie Kellner, Turner Broadcasting CEO (who also runs the WB) took a hard line. Kellner, who has a reputation as a tough negotiator, refused to pay over $1.8 million per episode. He also downplayed *Buffy's* importance to the WB, saying it was a niche show that appealed mainly to teens and certainly wasn't "irreplaceable."

The cast felt strongly about staying with the WB. After all, the WB had supported them and nurtured them from obscurity into one of the most praised shows on television. Sarah Michelle Gellar went as far as saying that she wouldn't play Buffy on any other network. Reminded that her contract with Fox had two more years to run and that she was obliged to play Buffy regardless of what network was airing the series, Gellar retracted her comments.

Whedon was furious, telling the *New York Daily News* that, "For Jamie Kellner to call it a teen show and dismiss his own product angers me. It doesn't breed love." For Whedon a key issue was the disrespect shown by Kellner, and he sent Kellner a letter complaining about the disparaging remarks.

Ultimately the WB lost the bidding to UPN, who offered $2.3 million per show. Whedon blamed the loss squarely on Kellner. "Jamie said 'I won't budge an inch,'" said Whedon, indicating that other top WB executives supported *Buffy*.

At the Television Critics Association Press Tour Gellar apologized for her comments during the negotiations. "What you have to understand is that for five years we had a home on the WB," Gellar says. "We had a place where we were supported, where we were able to make the show creatively the way we wanted to make it, and so the thought of making a move was scary."

UPN went out of its way to court its new prize, reportedly giving Gellar $8000 worth of Gucci items as a welcoming present. Gellar and the cast rapidly adjusted to their new home. Gellar said, "I'm nervous. I'm excited. UPN has been wonderful. They've said really wonderful things to make everybody feel incredibly welcome, and I think that's given us new excitement about the show. It's like getting to start fresh. It's like getting to show all of these new people the show we make, that we're all so incredibly proud of."

Joss Whedon also had kind words to say about UPN. "We really had some factors working in our favor," Whedon said. "UPN really came

Joss at *Buffy's* old home, the WB.

out swinging. They really promised and delivered a great deal of support. They put passion in it. Our fan base is not huge, but it is hugely loyal. I knew they would follow us."

Whedon expressed little concern that the move to UPN would cost Buffy its fan base. "I would like to think that most of my fan base is smart enough to use a remote."

At a Television Critics Association Press tour last year, witnesses were surprised to see Kellner approach Whedon, shake his hand and walk away. Whedon viewed this as an attempt to put the past behind them, particularly since *Angel* was still airing on the WB. Whedon feels the overture was sincere, not merely for appearances.

"I think he wanted to say, 'Let's put this behind us.' It's not like he did it in front of a crowd or photographers or anything. He just came up and I think he wanted to say, 'We've been doing business, there's been acrimony, but it's not personal. It's business.'"

So is the love back? Not exactly. Joss is ready to move on, but can never quite forget the insult to his baby. "You know, I didn't like the way the business was handled. I don't like doing business because I tend to take things personally. I do agree that I still have a show on the WB and he's still a part of the WB. I don't work with him day-to-day. If I did, then he and I would have to sit down and really iron things out. But in terms of what our relationship is—which is basically just peripheral to each other—I think we're fine.

Once *Buffy* formally made the move, the rumors began to run rampant that the show would be much sexier to lure in UPN's young male audience. There was also the belief that since UPN was paying so much more for it the show could afford a lot more special effects.

"There really isn't that big of a change because we have higher license fees," says Whedon. "Apart from the increases you accrue every year on a show, we are not looking at suddenly having a giant budget that we can do anything with. We're making the show exactly the way we were before. You know, we may have a little more leeway—we have more leeway than we would have, had we been forced to stay at the WB, and had no money and we'd have to use hand puppets."

So, after five years of kicking, punching and stabbing vampires, monsters and the undead into submission, Buffy plunged to her death through the gates of Hell. The program ended with a camera shot of Buffy's tombstone, which read, "She saved the world. A lot." As the image faded into the ending credits, a message appeared on the screen that said, "Five great years. We thank you." Joss said that when he saw the message at the end of the show, "I was actually moved. Then I said, 'Wait a minute.'

"The WB decided to pretend the series was ending," he added, calling the way the network played the finale "cheesy." Paul McGuire, a WB spokesman, said it was "a

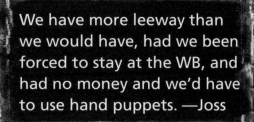

We have more leeway than we would have, had we been forced to stay at the WB, and had no money and we'd have to use hand puppets. —Joss

shame" if any *Buffy* fan had been misled. But he said the message of gratitude was a "sincere expression of thanks for five terrific years." Presumably, many *Buffy* viewers, even if confused at first, would be clued in by the fall, after the millions of dollars UPN spent to promote *Buffy's* return. In the end, Joss said, it was nothing personal—just business. "They're trying to protect their network and not help the other guy," he said.

"But basically we're right where we were, which is all that we were asking for. Fox is, you know, going to give us the increase we need, but not anything beyond that. And I think too much money spoils you; it

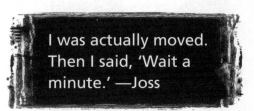

I was actually moved. Then I said, 'Wait a minute.' —Joss

lets you get lazy. If you can put spectacle on the air, you don't have to worry so much about story.

"It's important that people know that the WB never hindered us from doing the show the way we wanted to. We had some back and forth with them about certain scenes and certain ideas, but it was always collaboration. UPN basically stepped in and said, 'Make the show the way you've been making it.'

"And I'm not interested in pushing boundaries or smut or gore or anything like that. I'm interested in doing what we've been doing, which is sometimes dark and sometimes disturbing and sometimes sexy and all of that stuff. But you know that's not because I can get away with stuff. If you can just be sensational, then you don't have to tell the story right."

Spike

Unlike the Englishman he plays, James Marsters is 100 percent American. He was born in Greenville, California, and grew up in Modesto. From the early age of nine, Marsters knew he wanted to be an actor. His first role was as Eeyore in the fourth grade production of *Winnie the Pooh*.

Marsters went on to study at the Juilliard School in New York. Early in his career he starred in *The Tempest* and *Red Noses* at the Goodman Theater in Chicago. Not long after moving to the Pacific Northwest he landed a guest-starring role on *Northern Exposure*, which was his on-screen debut.

SUE SCHNEIDER / MOONGLOW PHOTOS

James Marsters, looking very Spikish.

This small success led him to believe he could find bigger and better things if he moved to Los Angeles. Soon he got the opportunity to audition for the role of Spike.

For the classically trained Marsters the idea of being on a show called *Buffy the Vampire Slayer* seemed a lark. He admits that he was one of the uncool before discovering what *Buffy* was all about.

"I have to admit I was one of those idiots," says Marsters. "When I got the word that they wanted me to audition for *Buffy the Vampire Slayer*, I was like 'I don't want to audition for *Buffy the...*' I'd never seen it, right?

"My agent said, 'Watch it and see. Don't give me an answer until you watch the show.' And I watched the show that night, and I got nervous because I wanted to be on that show so bad. It completely changed my mind. And it made me think about something, which is I think the name *Buffy the Vampire Slayer* almost dares you not to be cool enough to check it out. Almost like—and I've never said this to Joss, but I think almost like you don't want uncool people watching your show."

The audition went well. After several guest appearances Sarah Michelle Gellar thought it would be fun to have Marsters return as a full time player. She encouraged Joss to see what he could do about keeping Marsters on the series.

Meanwhile, Marsters was busy auditioning for other series including *Harsh Realm*, but the *Buffy* producers wooed him back. "I definitely am happy to be here," says Marsters. "You don't find characters like Spike every  day. There's a wealth of emotion he goes through on just about every episode and while it's hard work, it's also great fun. He's a very immature man; he was made a vampire at a young age and never got past that. I don't think he'll really ever understand what love really is, though he's certain he found it with Buffy."

> I've never said this to Joss, but I think almost like you don't want uncool people watching your show. —James Marsters

Marsters loves the fact that the writers constantly keep him on his toes. Each season as Spike evolves Marsters is learning about his character right along with the rest of us.

"No two seasons are alike at all. The characters go through completely different experiences every season. So whatever happened last season, turn it on its head, and … that's what you get next. But really, if you ask any male actor what he wants to do and he'll say bag chicks and kick butt, right? That's what we are used to seeing from these male macho characters. That's all guys want to do because they want the Bruce Willis kind of *Die Hard*, swinging from the rope with bullets thing. You know, what Marti and Joss come up with is infinitely more interesting than that. These are incredible stories that appeal to everyone from grandmas to kiddies."

Joss takes credit for Spike's distinctive look. "There's a little Billy Idol, a little Kiefer Sutherland in *The Lost Boys*, and every guy in a black coat. I really thought the peroxide would define his face better, though James does curse my name for the burning scalp."

But Marsters doesn't mind; he knows the Billy Idol look contributes a great deal to his fan appeal and transformation into semi-Scooby. "The coat works and the hair works. If the coat had been shorter or the hair had been black, I would have been dead."

Season six

Season six opens with Buffy's resurrection by Willow. Buffy comes back changed, disconnected from the world as a result of being called back from heaven. Meanwhile, Willow, in a not very subtle alcoholic analogy, falls deeper and deeper into the dark side of her magic. A troika of nerds is introduced as bad guys, but it's hard to take them seriously until they murder Katrina and, soon after, Tara. Willow reacts by heading into the dark side, killing Warren and ultimately deciding to destroy the world. In a very intense scene, she is stopped by Xander and his love for her, and the season ends with Willow in tears, embraced by Xander.

Joss was determined not to bring Buffy back without there being a price. In a brilliant move, we discover that Buffy was brought back from heaven, not hell. This is classic Joss because it's both shocking and, on reflection, so right.

"Buffy had to deal with the consequences of dying, going to heaven and coming back," Joss told the press while on a panel for the Academy of Television Arts & Sciences. "She had to learn how to live. When the house came down around Buffy as she slept with Spike that first time, it was a metaphor for her life. Her life was crashing down around her."

The nerd troika brought an element of humor to the largely dark season. According to an Internet posting by Joss, the troika, with their endless debates on sci-fi trivia, are modeled after the writing staff:

"It's SO PATHETIC how much the writing staff IS those guys, and I do include me. We're constantly having nerdtriv arguments and realizing they must go in scripts."

In another posting, Joss addresses Tara's death. Perhaps the most traumatic moment of the season was the death of Tara. Many fans objected and typically, Joss addressed this in an Internet posting:

"I killed Tara. Some of you may have been hurt by that. It [is] very unlikely it was more painful to you than it was to me. I couldn't even discuss it in story meetings without getting upset, physically. Which is why I knew it was the right thing to do. Because stories, as I have so often said, are not about what we WANT. And I knew some people

> I killed Tara. Some of you may have been hurt by that. —Joss

Danny Strong and Thomas Lenk, still looking pretty nerd

would be angry with me for destroying the only gay couple on the show, but the idea that I COULDN'T kill Tara because she was gay is as offensive to me as the idea that I DID kill her because she was gay. Willow's story was not about being gay. It was about weakness, addiction, loss . . . the way life hits you in the gut right when you think you're back on your feet. The course of true love never did run smooth, not on my show. (Only Dennis Franz has suffered more than my characters.) I love Amber and she knows it. Eventually, this story will end for all of them. Hers ended sooner.

Or did it . . .

Yeah, it did."

Season six had many great moments and some wonderful episodes (most notably *Once More With Feeling*) but fans complained about the overwhelming darkness of the season. With Buffy so disconnected, Willow fighting her magic addiction, Xander on the sidelines and Giles largely gone, fans struggled to build emotional links to the characters.

Joss felt strongly that the season, while dark and intense, was a success. "I'm not sure about the reception of [season six]," Joss says. "I've heard some people say, 'Oh, grrr-grr-grr-grr,' some season four-type rumblings. I'm *very* happy with it. I think we've hit exactly what we wanted to emotionally; where we are heading is devastating and fascinating to me. We all are just as excited as we could ever be. Even episodes that people don't necessarily think are landmark episodes are really solid, really well-crafted. So we're trying really hard.

"Last year I felt very good, but I also felt there was a kind of sameness to the through-line. This year, we've bounced back and forth between comedy and tragedy the way we used to and it feels really good. I'm probably the biggest fan. I have very few complaints."

Since Marti Noxon took the role of executive producer in season six, some of the criticism landed on her. But Joss resisted the implication that any weakness in season six was due to his lack of involvement or Noxon's leadership. While he only wrote and directed one episode, Joss maintains that he was intimately involved in every aspect of the production.

Fan sentiment was united on one point, however. *Once More With Feeling*, the musical Buffy episode, was brilliant. "I wanted to do something that was very traditional where people broke out into song and it seems like a natural thing," says Whedon. "It had a bit of a pop feel to it and I had a lot of help with it. Musicals are something that I've wanted to do for a long time, but had a tough time deciding how it could be done."

Joss with Nicholas Brendon and Amber Benson.

Joss told a group at the Academy of Television Arts & Sciences that the idea of how he could make it work came after watching an episode where Spike (James Marsters) was killing slayers through the ages. Marsters brought his guitar to the set one day and began singing and Anthony Head also sang.

He was surprised at the talent his cast had in belting out tunes. "I studied everybody's range," he says. "I know which of my cast members like to sing and which want to avoid it like the plague. I know who my heavy hitters are and I've geared the entire episode toward servicing that, so that everybody is comfortable.

"It terrified some of the actors…but pretty much everyone came on board and did a wonderful job. It's something I'm proud of in many ways. It is also one of the most difficult things I've ever produced."

"I was one of those who was horrified by the idea," says Hannigan. "It wouldn't have been so bad if I could carry a tune, but that isn't the case. I have to say Joss made it fun for us."

Whedon composed 11 original songs for the musical and even hired a professional choreographer and vocal coach to prepare his stars for their solos. "It's amazing that I lived to tell the tale," says Whedon, who spent six months shaping his vision into a reality. "When I tried to get Ali's (singing) range, she threw herself on the ground in my office and went, 'No!' It was actually kind of adorable. And Sarah (Michelle Gellar) wouldn't come up at all. Half of the cast was like, 'Whoo-hoo!' and the other half was like, 'Why do you punish us?' But, after six years, they've met every challenge I've ever thrown at them. So it's no surprise they pulled this off too."

> When I tried to get Ali's (singing) range, she threw herself on the ground in my office and went, 'No!' It was actually kind of adorable. —Joss

Hannigan was especially freaked out. "I begged, 'Can't Willow have laryngitis?'" she jests. "But it was beautiful. Now that I've seen the magic they can do in an engineering studio, I'm glad I got to do it." Trachtenberg successfully lobbied for a dancing role. "Joss wanted to write a whole song for Dawn," she reveals, "and I wasn't up for that." Joss therefore wrote a dancing number instead. "Dancing is definitely much more fun for me," she admits.

The show's star was also reluctant. "I'm not a singer, and I hated every moment of it," says Sarah Michelle Gellar. "It took something like 19 hours of singing and 17 hours of dancing in between shooting four other episodes." Gellar's initial impulse was to use a voice double, but she nixed that after hearing her songs. "I basically started to cry and said, 'You mean someone else is going to do my big emotional turning point for the season?'"

> I'm not a singer, and I hated every moment of it. —Sarah Michelle Gellar

Once More with Feeling contains 35 minutes of music and 13 minutes of dialogue. Each song is a seamless part of the overall story and advances the plotline. The episode, after extensive cutting, was eight minutes too long and Joss couldn't bring himself to cut any further. The executives liked it so much they agreed to let it run long.

"Buffy's first number, 'Going Through the Motions,' is a straight-up Disney production number—wicked Disney," says Whedon. But mostly "there are a lot of ballads, because the characters are going through emotions—and because I go to a sad place when I write." But there are exceptions, including Spike's rock number "Rest in Peace" and Xander and Anya's '30s-style song and dance number "I'll Never Tell" that, as Anya confesses, is "retro pastiche that's never going to be a breakaway pop hit."

The episode took six months to create. Joss had only learned to play the piano a few years before, and spent three months developing the score. He did it on his own, despite his novice compositional skills. There were three months of voice and dance lessons for the actors, and weeks of shooting around four other episodes. "It was a nightmare," says an exhausted Whedon. "The happiest nightmare I ever had."

The reviews were almost universally positive. *Entertainment Weekly* said that "Whedon has struck gold again in the best and most original episode since last season's 'Hush;' one would almost think this was a season premiere or cliffhanger because of what ensues."

According to *Salon*, "picking apart the technicalities of this *Buffy* episode... is the best way to miss the point of how beautifully it worked, how gracefully paced, clever and affecting it was. For one thing, Whedon figured out how to make the music a seamless part of the action, by working it into the plot as a joke.

"But *Once More with Feeling* works mostly because the musical numbers are keyed right into the heartbeat of the show, a show whose mythology, by now, in the midst of the sixth season, is so rich and deliciously Byzantine that you could almost design a college course around it. There was joy and lightness in *Once More with Feeling*, particularly the sequence where Tara and Willow, the show's Wiccan lesbian lovers, cavort in an almost insanely sunny park, twirling about in medieval-looking frocks. The scene ends in the couple's bedroom, with Tara gently levitating inches above the bed as Willow hovers somewhere just below the frame, one of the best metaphors for the bliss of oral sex I've seen on any screen, small or large."

Buffy pushes sexual boundaries in season six with a number of intense scenes between Buffy and Spike, especially Spike's attempted rape of Buffy in *Seeing Red*. Noxon and Whedon decided to include this scene as a reminder to the many fans who seem to have decided Spike was one of the good guys. "People kept saying, 'You know, Spike's a really great guy.' I'm like, 'I know, he's come a long way. But in his heart of hearts, he still doesn't quite know the difference between right and wrong,'" Noxon

In the middle of Santa Monica you'll find a grouping of tin buildings that make up the set of *Buffy*. When Joss says they built the whole thing out of a bunch of tin huts, he means it. This isn't your typical television lot. Within the humble exterior lies what looks like a street in any small town. There's a cinema on the corner and a Mexican restaurant across the street. If it weren't for the "Magic Box" sign on one of the storefronts, you would never know that it's Sunnydale.

A great many of the scenes for *Buffy* are shot inside this huge faux-cinema; it holds the entire downstairs of the house where Buffy lives. The front of the house has been built to look just like the original home located in Torrance, California—this is called a second face. It's used so that the show doesn't have to shoot exteriors on location. The crew of *Buffy* started doing exterior shots on this lot after wearing out their welcome in Torrance while shooting the season three finale. That final explosion scene set off half the car alarms in town!

It's a little eerie to cross the threshold into the home of Buffy Summers. I'd never imagined how striking an experience it would be to witness the place where the magic of *Buffy* occurs. Being an entertainment reporter has its perks; I was afforded the opportunity to touch the worn chairs on the front porch, examine the books stacked in mission-style cases and sit in the dining room where the Scoobies spend so much time hanging out.

I stepped into Buffy's living room. There stood the very couch where Joyce died in "The Body." I took a few steps deeper into the house and found myself in the hallway where Buffy vomited after she found her mother dead, and hurried on into the homey kitchen which leads to the dining room. I peeked around the right corner to find the front entryway and the staircase that should lead up to Buffy's bedroom—but the upstairs of the house is actually a part of a different set, in the back of the huge soundstage.

I made another round about the downstairs set, taking in little details that comprise Buffy's living space—knickknacks, pictures and furniture that I've seen via a cathode ray tube for years and could now actually touch and see. I then left the first story of the house for the other side of the soundstage, where I got to examine the upstairs section of the Summers' home.

I was immediately drawn to Dawn's bedroom, a pink, purple and green teen haven. Teen magazines litter the floor and furniture, and there's a stuffed Scooby Doo tucked away in the closet. (Wonder where that came from?) Puzzles and books fill the bookcase, along with a groovy lava lamp. Photos of a much younger Dawn—a Dawn the audience never saw—grace the walls, and notebooks are stacked on the desk next to a wizard snow globe and a large framed picture of Joyce.

There are more pictures of Joyce in the hallway leading to Willow and Tara's room. The walls are loaded with family photos, pictures of the Summers' women smiling as if there were no danger lurking in Sunnydale, no Hellmouth just down the road.

The comfortable sparse decor of Willow and Tara's bedroom is violently interrupted by the still-broken pane of glass and the bloodstain on the carpet. Though I know it's fake blood, the room still gives me chills. The walls seem to contain a deep sadness, and I think I can now understand a bit better what drove Willow over the edge at the end of season six.

The upstairs bathroom is in need of a good cleaning. Evidently someone's too busy fighting demons to scrub the white and black vinyl floor. I took a second to remember Spike attempting the rape of Buffy in this room just before his soul was restored. I then made my way to Buffy's room.

There's so much to see in this bedroom, where many of the props were taken from the sets of other shows. There's a small little case that has been taken from the show *Space Above and Beyond* and a sticker on her mirror that says *Professional Murder*. I couldn't resist sitting on her bed and looking at all the pictures of Buffy with other characters in the show. It just felt amazing to be sitting right in the middle of one of the only sets to survive since season one (the Bronze set is also still used)—for six years fans have watched Buffy grow up in this very room, in this very house.

I wanted the chance to see more, and got a distant view of the cemetery where Buffy does so much slaying. I saw a set in the process of being built across the soundstage—it looks like they're rebuilding the high school. I also got to venture into Spike's crypt. The sturdy-looking room appears to be solid concrete, but mostly consists of plastic, Styrofoam and plywood. Spike's TV (for daily episodes of *Passions*) is missing, but his chair sits by the door next to some filthy cobwebs. The melted candles in elaborate stands finish off the Goth dwelling that Spike calls home.

I also took a peek into Xander's apartment. Everything in his cozy abode screams kitsch, from the Tiki bar (complete with hula girls) to the *Star Trek* figurines. A large basket of laundry and an ironing board take up a corner of his bedroom and there's clutter everywhere: *Fantastic Four* comics, hockey magazines, hockey sticks and surf boards. Looks like Xander is missing Anya in more ways than one.

Time got away from me while I explored the world that had come straight from Joss' vivid imagination—it was time to interview a couple of the actors who worked on the show. Time for me to step outside of Joss' surreal world and find out more about what made his vision a reality.

said of the episode. Buffy and Spike's relationship had a clear sado-masochistic component. Of course, these weren't the first sado-masochistic scenes in *Buffy*. There were a number of others, most notably Drusilla's torture scene with Giles and vampire Willow's playtime with the "puppy" (the alternate universe Angel).

> I know, he's come a long way. But in his heart of hearts, he still doesn't quite know the difference between right and wrong.
> —Marti Noxon

In a classic Whedon move, the nerd troika turn out to be a fake, while Willow winds up as the season's "big bad." "Her magic gets out of control," says Hannigan. "Things go awry and it's frightening." Sighing, she adds, "I don't want to be bad! Nobody will like me. That's the hardest thing to get over as an actress. What if they don't like me?"

But Hannigan has fun with Willow's evil side as well. "You know, there's this power that comes to you when you just sort of let loose and play the bad girl," says Hannigan. "During that time Willow was doing what she thought was best for everyone, and she didn't see it as evil in any way. She brought Buffy back from the dead, not to punish her, but to free her from some weird alternate dimension she thought Buffy was in. Things did get a bit out of hand and the power went to her head, but she's paid for her crimes.

"I was grateful that Joss and the gang gave me a chance to show a different side of Willow. Now we know she always has that lurking underneath and it gives her a little more depth."

In the last scene of the season, it's revealed that Spike's soul is restored. It's not clear whether Spike knew this would happen, but it's abundantly clear that Whedon has interesting things planned for season seven.

Season seven

In season seven, which was to be the last, Joss promised a lighter tone, and at the beginning of the season he delivered. "[Season six] has been fantastic, but it has had a darker tone. To be honest, some of the episodes depressed the hell out of me. This is where we wanted to go . . . into the dark of the woods. But next year is going to be very different. We're going back to our original mission statement. Back to the joy of female empowerment. This year was about adult life and relationships–and making really, really bad decisions. Next year will still be scary and different and strange, but it will be more of a positive outlook. People will stop abandoning Dawn. Willow won't be a junky anymore. Buffy won't be dead."

Season seven was something of a reunion, with Whedon bringing back favorite characters including Faith, Glory and Drusilla. Giles returned to do twelve of the episodes, some of which were shot in England. It rained the entire time the crew was in England, but shooting proceeded nevertheless. "We got the footage. Tony and Ally are great and that's England in the background so I'm happy," Joss says.

Joss was thrilled to get back to England, this time not as a shy high school student, but as a major Hollywood producer. "I just always wanted to go back over there. Because I only had to fly one person out they let me do it. I already had Tony there and it just made sense for Willow's character to have spent her time under Giles' watch and guidance."

As for the storyline for season seven, Whedon remained coy throughout. "I can only tell you a little bit," he said before the last season began. "This is something I've been sort of gearing towards since the very beginning of the show. It's a question of bringing it onto a much larger scale and at the same time making it much more personal and much more personal to Buffy herself. This year [season six] was a chance to let the other characters [shine.]

". . . The big climactic scene [was] between Xander and Willow, and that was because, as characters and as actors, they'd earned that opportunity. And I thought it was right for them to sort of be the spokespeople for what was going on at the end there. But next year Buffy will be much less peripheral to the climax. The climax will be the biggest thing we've ever done."

Whedon added, "You know, every year it might be the end. Except, actually, this year [season six]. This year I really did sort of leave it up in the air. You could have said this could have been an end, but the [cliffhanger] with Spike and the thing on Angel [leaving Angel at the bottom of the ocean], this was sort of the exception to the rule.

> The big climactic scene [was] between Xander and Willow, and that was because, as characters and as actors, they'd earned that opportunity. —Joss

Joss with real-life couple Hannigan and Alexis Denisof. Can it be only coincidence that both Willow and Wesley have flirted with the dark side?

But I am looking for closure next year…because we're making a more positive statement. This year was just about surviving the year. Sometimes the audience felt that actually it's their chore too. What? You don't want to be depressed all the time like me? I don't understand. But next year is something that's a lot more positive and definitive. And in that it has to end with an exclamation point, not a question mark."

Joss has also hinted that there may be a *Buffy*—*Angel* crossover episode, if the networks (the WB particularly) overcome their animosity. It's not clear yet whether this will happen.

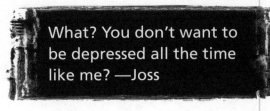

What? You don't want to be depressed all the time like me? —Joss

Critics and Emmys

Critics, like fans, have embraced *Buffy the Vampire Slayer*.

"*Buffy* sounds like goofy kids' show to most people, but it has depth, layers and texture that some alleged 'adult' series could only hope for," says Rob Owen, a TV editor for the *Pittsburgh Post-Gazette*.

"Joss is a master of everything, by which I mean he's equally adept at emotional drama and character comedy, action sequences and quiet romantic moments. The show has suffered this season [six] from his lack of day-to-day involvement. The show no longer has the balance it once had.

"That being said, this season's 'Once More with Feeling' musical episode is one of my favorites. 'Hush,' which has 20 minutes with no dialogue, is probably my all-time favorite episode, which he wrote and directed.

Joss is a master of everything, by which I mean he's equally adept at emotional drama and character comedy, action sequences and quiet romantic moments. —Rob Owen

"Joss is just a very creative guy. He's created a unique group of characters and allowed them to grow and mature and evolve throughout the course of the show. He has the sensibility of a fan, something not often found in TV producers, which is what endears him to the fan community. He's a sci-fi geek at heart making shows for other sci-fi geeks."

Tom Walter, the television critic for the Memphis paper, concurs. "Whedon is a great example of getting a second chance and running at it, and a great example of how television is much friendlier to writers than the movies are," Walters explains. "He was able to take a lackluster movie (whose fault was that—studio interference or whatever—probably doesn't matter anymore) and turn it into a gem of a series.

Marti Noxon, *Buffy* executive producer and "parking ticket lady," clutches her Saturn.

SUE SCHNEIDER / MOONGLOW PHOTOS

"... Early on, *Buffy* was simply amazing. It took teen alienation and angst about as far as it could go—name me a bigger outsider than a vampire killer—but did it with rare humor and panache. This was a sophisticated, witty, well-written, well-cast, well-acted show from the start, one that didn't hit you over the head with its metaphors."

So why is it that the show gets so little respect when it comes the big awards shows? Is it the genre or the teen orientation? Is it the quirky name?

"I don't mean to be rude but, sometimes people look at a title and make a decision. I know when Joss first was creating the show people didn't want it named *Buffy the Vampire Slayer* because they were afraid it would turn people off," says star Sarah Michelle Gellar.

"This show is the most wonderful mix of brilliant, witty writing and phenomenal performances and evolving stories. And if people turn their head to it and say they won't watch it like they would watch the *Power Rangers*, to me that really is just ignorance," says Gellar.

> This was a sophisticated, witty, well-written, well-cast, well-acted show from the start, one that didn't hit you over the head with its metaphors.
> —Tom Walter

"There are some people who never take genre shows seriously," says Whedon. "It's a prejudice that I'll never understand. But because anything to do with fantasy just turns them off and anything that's humorous must not be meaningful. So this year they are all going to be doctors so we can get some Emmys."

Oh, there's that Emmy word. The show has been nominated but it's still a sore subject among the cast and crew.

"But we specifically—we don't make the show to win awards. The reason we stayed on the air in our first 13 was because we had this incredibly strong fan base, this Internet fan base, and fans that would write into magazines. They're the reason we make the show, and that's the accolades that I think we all, as a group, look for," Gellar says.

"We have received nominations in the past and that was rewarding, and so you sort of go 'maybe that will happen again.' But the fact of the matter is with a name like *Buffy the Vampire Slayer* you're never going to be Emmy bait. So it's sort of—it doesn't really affect the way we do the show. It's not like were are going to say 'let's make a very special episode, let's figure out an Emmy theme, what do they like, what do they go for?' It's not relevant to us," says Whedon.

"Also, I said this before, but I think that the voting population for the Emmys are not the people who watch our show," says Noxon. "And so much of it is the shows you watch and talk about with your friends and peers about. I think in general, the newer people to the WGA (Writers Guild Association) and the SAG (Screen Actors Guild) and all of these different organizations don't know they can join the academy. So until there's a younger constituent…"

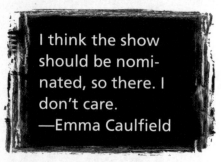

I think the show should be nominated, so there. I don't care.
—Emma Caulfield

Emma Caulfield (Anya) steps in, "I don't think it's very political to say it, but I'm going to say it. I think the show should be nominated, so there. I don't care. We have the best writers working for us. We have an amazing creator, show-runner, I mean all the way around. We have an amazing cast, one of the most talented ensemble casts put together, and it would be nice to be nominated. I think the show should be nominated. So there."

"What bothers me the most is that the cast isn't nominated," says Whedon. "We are a genre show, but I think they are ignored because they are young and they don't get the recognition they deserve. I defy you to show me a better ensemble than these guys," he says pointing to all of his cast members.

Whedon even paid for a campaign designed to help the show win an Emmy, but to no avail. "I feel like I just spent a lot of money trolling for a compliment that I didn't get," Joss now says with regret.

What's Next?

With season seven as the last for *Buffy*, the big question was, "What happens next?" Gellar's contract was up at the end of season seven, and she didn't want to continue with the show.

"It was so sad when I had to tell Joss that I really didn't want to do this anymore," said Gellar. "It had nothing to do with wanting to go off and make movies, I'm just tired. This is a very physical role and I want to do something else."

Joss, who had signed an eight-figure production deal with Fox, was being pulled in several directions, so everyone decided that season seven would be the last for *Buffy*, "As we know it now," Joss added.

There had been some discussion that the series would continue, but without Gellar. Joss talked at length about his desire to create a show for several of the remaining characters. "We have some strong and very talented people with on *Buffy*, so we are definitely planning to use them on a future project." There was some speculation that the introduction of Dawn at the beginning of season five (at 15, one year younger than Buffy in season one) was a hedge against Gellar's possible departure. Another alternative was the return of Faith, but much to Joss's chagrin, Eliza Dushku signed on to do another new series with Fox. Dushku did appear in the final five episodes of season seven of *Buffy* (and three episodes of *Angel*), but she couldn't come back as the slayer who saves the day because she had her own show on another network.

Throughout season seven Whedon teased the idea that a new slayer, out of nowhere, could come in to take Gellar's place, but he continued to keep the audience guessing as there was never a sure fit.

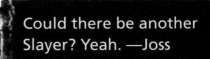

Could there be another Slayer? Yeah. —Joss

"Could there be another Slayer?" Whedon said. "Yeah. But you are talking about a radically different show..."

A third possibility was the end of the TV show, but its resurrection as a series of movies (a la *Star Trek*). Joss expressed interest in a movie, as did many of the cast, but insists this will have to wait until the series ends. Gellar wasn't on board with the idea of a movie. She's expressed skepticism that a second *Buffy* movie would do better than the first. "You know, I don't ever say never," Gellar says. "But right now it's too close. I'm tired and I want to take rest." So the fate of any *Buffy* movie is still up in the air.

Before the season seven finale the rumors were flying. Joss and his cohorts were diligent about not sharing information. Head told reporters, "I know what he's got in mind, but I ain't going to tell you. It's brilliant." Joss later said, "Look, no one really wants to know what is going to happen. It ruins the surprise for everyone. You might think you want to know, but you don't. I have an idea of what's going to happen next, but I could change my mind tomorrow."

Angel 6

> "Angel was the one character who is bigger than life in the same way that Buffy was . . . a kind of superhero."
>
> —Joss Whedon

The WB launched *Angel*, a *Buffy* spin-off, in the fall of 1999. *Angel* was set in the *Buffy* universe, but was intended to be very different in tone. *Angel* was aimed at twentysomethings looking for meaning in a confusing world. The concept was film-noirish, and originally focused on Angel as a private eye, solving a supernatural case each week.

Critical to *Angel*'s success was finding an identity that was clearly distinct from *Buffy*, while still appealing to *Buffy* fans. "When we conceived *Angel*, we knew we wanted a much darker show and for it to be different in tone from *Buffy*," says Whedon. "It's inherently different because the star is David, but at the same time we didn't want to do the same thing we had done before. It

> When we conceived *Angel*, we knew we wanted a much darker show and for it to be different in tone from *Buffy*. —Joss

was an opportunity for us to move in a new direction. The show is set in Los Angeles because there are a lot of demons in LA, and a wealth of stories to be told.

"We also wanted to take the show a little older and have the characters deal with demons in a much different way. Angel has a business that he runs with his friends. And he has relationships with different demons. We learn that not all demons are bad. The show complements *Buffy* in a lot of ways, but they couldn't be more different.

"Buffy is always the underdog trying to save the world, but Angel is looking for redemption. It's those two things that creatively make the shows different."

"Well, there's no denying, of course, that *Angel* grew out of *Buffy*," says Greenwalt, coproducer of *Angel*. "But even from . . . the first time David came to *Buffy* . . . we were always discovering new things. I'll never forget the first episode . . . Buffy discovers that he's a vampire and they kiss for the first time, and it was just incredible. You know David brought so much of that to the role. David always represented something scary and then something occasionally funny, which are all of the things we like to do. But when we spun the show off originally, our notion was this will be a really dark, gritty, urban show.

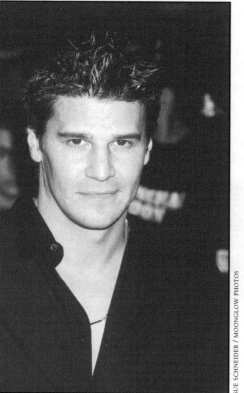

David Boreanaz, looking a bit Angelus-like.

"Our show takes place in the big city, the characters seem older, they seem more mature, it seems more like the travails of your twenties. It just seems meaner and leaner to me, this show. But certainly there are many elements . . . I was going to say that are stylistically the same, but that's not the right word. Something in the way that Joss finds the core of things, and just when you think something wonderful is going to happen, something terrible happens and vice versa."

For David Boreanaz (Angel) having his own show has been both exciting and frightening. In the beginning he had talked with Gellar about the pressures of being the lead and what that means, but it didn't prepare him for the burden he would bear. Whereas in *Buffy* it was Gellar who was in most every scene, now it was Boreanaz's turn to be the focus of almost every frame. It meant a lot of hard work and long hours.

Whedon knew from the first season of

Buffy that Boreanaz had something special. It was watching Boreanaz in a season-two episode of *Buffy* that convinced Whedon that he could carry his own show. He wasn't the only candidate; Whedon also felt that Hannigan, for example, had the appeal to headline a show. But the character of Angel was special. "Angel was the one character who is bigger than life in the same way that Buffy was," says Whedon. "A kind of superhero. And I knew–as the dark, mysterious love interest–that he had the potential for a breakout

> Something in the way that Joss finds the core of things, and just when you think something wonderful is going to happen, something terrible happens and vice versa.
> —David Greenwalt

character. But I also knew he had the potential to go away after a couple of episodes. But then we found David Boreanaz and he doesn't seem to be able to go away at all," laughs Joss.

To bring a sense of continuity to the show, Joss and Greenwalt decided to bring the character Cordelia Chase, played by Charisma Carpenter, with Angel. She initially helped the vampire set up Angel Investigations, and provided much of the humor in the seriously dark show.

"You know, it's a little scary when you are moving from a successful show to something that may or may not do well," says Carpenter. "For me though, it was a no-brainer. There wasn't much more they could do with

SUE SCHNEIDER / MOONGLOW PHOTOS

Charisma Carpenter plays the ever evolving Cordelia.

my character on *Buffy*. If Cordelia stayed in Sunnydale, she would never grow. I was flattered when Joss and the guys asked if I would be interested in doing the new show. They told me some of what they had planned for my character and I just jumped on board.

"I liked the idea at first that Cordelia was going off to be a small fish in a big pond and she doesn't have a clue on how to survive in the entertainment world," says Carpenter. "We learned a lot about her character in those early episodes of *Angel* that we never knew before. Look how much she has grown over the years since *Angel* began. I certainly didn't see any of this coming—oh that's funny, because Cordelia probably could have seen it."

Whedon was intimately involved in every aspect of the show's launch, but it was clear from the outset that *Buffy* would continue to dominate his time. Joss Whedon and David Greenwalt coproduced *Angel*, and Joss, while trying to direct one episode per year, left the day-to-day management of the series to Greenwalt. But, Greenwalt insists, Joss is always involved.

"Our offices are close," Greenwalt emphasizes. "When we were on *Buffy,* my office was right next to Joss's, and now I'm downstairs in the same building with all of the other *Angel* people. And there's not a major thing that happens on the show that isn't something that he and I haven't discussed. And usually it's some surprise."

Gellar was a bit apprehensive about the spin-off, concerned about losing Whedon's direction, not to mention one of her favorite costars. "Joss is our show," says Gellar, "I mean this is him. And when he first told me that he had this idea, I cried. I was excited for David. I was so excited at the concept that Joss would have a chance to tell more stories, because that's what he does so brilliantly. But I was concerned, because I don't think we know how to make our show without him.

"Joss assured me that no matter how famous and busy he becomes he will be involved in our show. As long as I know that, I'm happy. And as for David, he is amazing actor and I miss working with him. At the same time I think he's doing a fantastic job with his show."

"There's a certain amount of pressure that comes with having to be the lead in your own show," says Boreanaz, "but it isn't like I'm doing it all by myself. We have this great cast and crew who are a huge part of what we are doing. So I feel some pressure, but only in that I want us all to do well."

The show has been a learning process for Boreanaz. "I've learned that kindness is more than a loving word, that extending one's hand to your fellow workers and getting through [the] day together is [important]. Shooting a television show can be very difficult and at times it can really wear on yourself as a person. And if you keep reminding yourself that it is a job and you show up together as a team and as a whole, that . . . you can prevail and get through the day or the eight days that it takes to shoot one episode.

"Since I arrived on *Buffy* as a recurring character, I've grown considerably as a person on the inside from the help of my friends and my family. And now that I'm married, I have a beautiful wife and a child.

Yes, he's married. David Boreanaz and his real-life wife Jaime Bergman (*Son of a Beach*).

Life has been very good to me and I look at that as a reward in itself. So along the way you learn, and as long as I keep learning with the show and struggling, trying to find something new every day with it, then it's more exciting for me to show up. The hardest part is showing up. Getting out of bed for anybody is hard, and driving to work–well, actually I get picked up. Getting into the passenger seat is difficult," he laughs.

Greenwalt credits Boreanaz with helping him keep his temper. "David is always reminding me that we all have a purpose here, we are all here for [a] reason and it all fits together in a way that you can't always see, and he's actually helped me keep my temper a few times."

"It's important to stay grounded," says Boreanaz. "You have to keep reminding yourself that it's a show. We're here to entertain and put out the best product that we possibly can. And on our show, we set the bar extremely high. Sometimes I set it high and get frustrated with myself, but that's just the type of person I am."

The first season was a tough one for everyone involved. The show was still trying to find itself creatively and though they had many hits, there were also a lot of misses. The balance between dark and light was often difficult for the writers to define, and there were many times when the show was overly dark.

As noted, *Angel* was initially conceived as film-noirish, with each episode setting up and resolving a detective case. This format, while interesting, abandoned some of *Buffy's* core strengths, notably the focus on relationships and the multi-episode story arcs.

There were also problems with the two creators, Greenwalt and Whedon, being stretched too thin. They were both working sixteen hours a day, six days a week, and while they felt like they were telling good stories, they were the first to admit there were problems. In the middle of the season, Whedon, Greenwalt, and all of the writers were thrown into meetings to find out what it was the show was missing. The network execs, who were patient with Joss in the past, insisted that they fix the show and do so immediately.

"It wasn't like, 'Oh my God, it's the end of the world,'" Joss relates. "It was the network telling us that we needed to make an adjustment, and David Greenwalt and I saying, 'We wish we disagreed with you, but we don't.'

"It was a matter of getting back to what we told the network we would do," says Whedon. "We created this world for Angel but at the same time we had to make the stories something people could relate to in some way.

"We knew when things weren't working," Whedon says. "It was a matter of sitting down and doing a bit more planning. We had to take a hard look at the first year and see what worked, and what didn't. Then we had to make some decisions about what type of show we wanted to put out there."

Some cast changes were made and new characters were brought into Angel Investigations. Doyle (Glenn Quinn) who was one of the original members of Angel's entourage was written out and Cordelia inherited his demon powers. They also brought in Alexis Denisof, who played Wesley Wyndam-Pryce on *Buffy*, at the end of the season.

When they began the show, they had wanted to do an anthology where each episode wrapped up a case. Unfortunately, the viewers were more invested in the characters and the mythology. So, the show began to take a turn for the better when the characters were better developed, with multi-episode story arcs and a stronger mythology for the series. The writers felt they had a strong through-line with the Wolfram and Hart story, so they decided to make the lawyers a part of the show's mythology.

Charles Gunn (J. August Richards) was added to the investigative team and the writers brought back some old *Buffy* favorites, Darla (Julie Benz) and Drusilla (Juliet Landau).

SUE SCHNEIDER / MOONGLOW PHOTOS

Gunn (J. August Richards) brings a touch of normalcy and romance to the *Angel* team.

"We were sitting around talking about the show with some of the writers and producers," says Joss, "and the idea came up to bring Darla back as a human. It was something we all immediately jumped on and knew would work within the show. That relationship and Angel turning to his dark side helped to define the season. We still weren't exactly where we wanted to be, but I don't think you ever are 100 percent happy with anything you do."

"Having five [regular] characters really allows for more complex stories to come out of the characters, rather than coming from the outside, which is where we *thought* they would come from when we first started the show," says Joss. Then we started looking for another female, and Amy Acker [Fred] walked into the room and just stole the hearts of every single person who saw her. Actually, she hasn't given them back yet. I'm afraid when she does she's gonna give out the wrong ones and I'm gonna get someone else's."

Amy Acker—is she still keeping Joss's heart?

"It's progressed considerably," says Boreanaz of the show. "From what it was in the beginning and how it was, you know, kind of searching and what were these characters actually doing in the big city and in Los Angeles.

". . . everything just fell into place from day one of season three. The characters are all strong, they each have their own identity and they're each going their own paths, but all of those paths are going to the core. . . ."

Season one ends with restoration of Darla (killed in season one of *Buffy*) and the destruction of Angel's cramped apartment/office.

Angel kicks into gear in season two, which opens with a new, more expansive set and a restored (and now human) Darla. The story features a turn towards evil for Angel, his epiphany, and a Darla-Drusilla rampage. According to Greenwalt, Joss came up with many of the season's twists. "That's one of the things I've loved about working with Joss, which is, 'Let's do this. What if he locks all the lawyers in the room and lets these vampire girls kill them? What if he fires these people? What if they go to another dimension?' You know, there's always something new. It's not the same formula every week and that, for me, is what keeps it exciting," says Greenwalt.

> Amy Acker [Fred] walked into the room and just stole the hearts of every single person who saw her. Actually, she hasn't given them back yet. I'm afraid when she does she's gonna give out the wrong ones and I'm gonna get someone else's. —Joss

Julie Benz and Juliet Landau, looking lovely and dangerous. Would you care to be locked in a room with them?

Season two ends with a four-episode story arc that takes Angel, Cordelia, Wesley, Gunn, and the Host to the Host's native dimension, a hellish place featuring human slavery and the absence of music. These episodes put Angel in a black-and-white world in which being a hero is much more straightforward. Speaking before it aired, Joss said, "I couldn't be more excited about it. In this world, Angel can walk in the sunlight, so he's loving life. He's a hero, but then, of course, he learns there's a price to pay." Never one to mince words, Whedon added, "I'll go on record in saying it's a gay romp."

> That's one of the things I've loved about working with Joss, which is, 'Let's do this. What if he locks all the lawyers in the room and lets these vampire girls kill them? What if he fires these people? What if they go to another dimension?' —David Greenwalt

These episodes are notable for showcasing Joss's first acting role as Loren's dancing brother, Numfar. This came about when Whedon jokingly showed Greenwalt and Minear his idea for the crazy dance and the producers thought he looked just stupid enough to be great in the part.

Before he knew it, the decision was made to put makeup on Joss and turn him into the grotesque and not-too-talented dancing fool Numfar. "No, no, it was just a crazy thing we did and it was funny," laughs Whedon. "I had a little fun making myself look like an idiot. The makeup took two and half hours, but the idiot part was fairly simple."

> I'll go on record in saying it's a gay romp. —Joss

Joss confesses he has the acting bug but is trying to be realistic about his limitations. "I've always had it, and I think it's part of being a writer and a director. It's knowing how you want things to be played. But I don't have the face—that's the problem—and I don't want the giant ego. I don't want to become Kevin Costner, singing on the soundtrack to *The Postman*. The acting bug mostly [came] from doing our weekly Shakespeare readings."

Nevertheless, it's hard to shake the bug. "Well, you know, I keep saying

Joss demonstrates his acting talents when captured by *Star Wars* storm troopers.

to Greenwalt, 'Yeah, this story's interesting, Angel's going through a lot, [but] what's the Numfar of it?" Joss says, sounding very much like Xander. "What's Numfar learning? What's Numfar dancing about? Let's really examine the important things!"

"We started the show with three characters and we've sort of grown each year," says Greenwalt. "Look at *Buffy* over there. They have, like, forty-one regulars and you can't get in the room when everyone is together," jokes Greenwalt. "Again it's a direct influence from Joss for our own show. We like to get

> I don't want to become Kevin Costner, singing on the soundtrack to *The Postman*. —Joss

new people in the mix, and we'll see if we can add a new one [regular character] every year. We've done it so far. The bigger the family gets, the more the merrier in a way. People come and go on the show and I love having certain characters go back and forth. It gives us more people with more problems and issues to work with."

Joss with former executive producer David Greenwalt.

Long before any of the major characters hit the small screen, they were rolling around in Joss's head somewhere. The idea for Fred (a physicist stranded in an alternate dimension) had been bubbling for a while when he met Acker. "There was just something in the way she read the part that I just knew she was Fred," says Whedon. "She has a great ability to be very serious and do comedy in the same breath." Acker would be a series regular in season three.

"I'm still so excited just to have this job," Acker enthuses. "I feel so lucky just to work with people like Joss. Anyone who comes to visit us on set is like, 'This is amazing, you all like each other so much.' We just have the best dynamic and I think that helps the show."

"Then you have Gunn," Whedon added, "who is the guy with the street smarts. The addition of the character and J. August Richards brought a new dimension to our little group. There's a definite vibe between his character and Fred, and that could turn into something long-term. Or as long-term as we can get."

Andy Hallett, who plays Lorne the Host, is a longtime friend of Whedon's. They've spent a number of hours together hanging out in seedy karaoke bars across LA. (Yes, Joss can sing; he and Kai Cole can be heard on the *Once More with Feeling* album.) Joss came up with an idea for a demon club owner who could read people's hearts while they were singing. Hallet was surprised when he learned the character was based on him, and even more so when Joss suggested he audition for the part.

Lorne is based on Andy, but that didn't guarantee he would get the job. When they began casting for the part, Whedon asked that the producers see his friend and he left the ultimate decision up to them.

"He told me I could audition, but he didn't promise me anything. It was my first time to go out for something like this and they made me work for it," Hallet told BBC.com in an interview. "This wasn't an easy job to get, even though the character was based on me. I thought it would be only for a few episodes and then ended up getting seventeen out of twenty-two that third season."

In season three, *Angel* really hits its stride with a complex plot line featuring Angel's nemesis Holtz, a pregnant Darla, and, ultimately, Angel's confrontation with his suddenly grown-up son. In season three, *Angel* proved that, like *Buffy*, it was ready to rapidly evolve and enter new territory. "What I do like about the show is that it does keep changing and we are full of surprises and people come and go as they do in real life," says Greenwalt. "People have babies and other things happen. People fall in love and people move forward. The idea that Angel and Cordelia would have feelings for each other, it scared us all and it sort of appeared out of the material. And we said, 'No, but Buffy'–and he [Joss] was like, 'People move on. You have to move forward all of the time.'"

Whedon was the force behind some of the key emotional turning points, including making Angel a father. Coincidentally (or perhaps not), Joss's wife became pregnant with their first child during this season. "He needed something to connect to emotionally. Plus, I just love the idea of this embarrassing effect of a one-night stand." Joss also decided to quickly bring the child to adulthood. "What are you going to do? Have a baby running around? I don't think so. There were advantages.

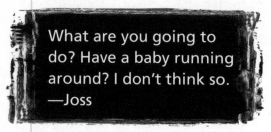

What are you going to do? Have a baby running around? I don't think so.
—Joss

He got to have a baby. He got to have his child taken away. And then he got to have a full-grown son. That's the beauty of it being a fantasy show."

"I thought *Angel* was particularly good this year [2001—2002 season]," says Professor Basinger. "It took them a while to find what this was supposed to be. The story line with the son moved *Angel* to a whole new level. I've found it interesting to watch how this show has evolved. Joss only writes and directs a few episodes a year, but you always know which ones are his. He has a distinct style and a way of storytelling that no one else can duplicate."

As much as his cast and producers love him, they still like to give him a difficult time. Greenwalt is quick to point out that there are times when even he wonders where Whedon's mind has gone. The cast and crew were shocked when Joss wanted to take the show to the ballet (*Waiting in the Wings*, written and directed by Whedon). It was something Joss had wanted to do for a long time, and it became one of the standout episodes of all time.

It was Acker's favorite as well. "By far my favorite episode was Joss's episode *Waiting in the Wings*. Even though no one gets to see it in the episode, Alexis and I got to do a beautiful dance number. I hadn't danced for eight years before that. I had told him that I had taken ballet for fourteen years, but I didn't tell him which fourteen years of my life [it] had been.

"Joss is [in] love with the ballet and I guess he felt the show wasn't quite gay enough yet," laughs Greenwalt.

"I just want everyone to know that Angel is not gay," laughs Boreanaz, "not that there's anything wrong with that. But Angel is not gay. Are we clear on that?"

"I wasn't sure what to think when Joss told me what he wanted to do with the ballet episode," says Greenwalt. "But that's just Joss, and it worked. I know that I should never have any doubts about what comes out of that brain of his. But you have to admit that it was a strange idea, one of the more different ones we've had on the show."

The fans fell in love with the characters too. At the end of the third season, the show was doing better than ever on the WB and was renewed for another year. Unfortunately, the fate of many of the characters was uncertain. Cordelia floated up to the powers that be. Angel was trapped in a box and dumped in the ocean by his son. Wesley was on a binge of self-destruction. Lorne the Host went off to find a new life, and Gunn and Fred were left alone wondering what happened to everyone.

> Joss is [in] love with the ballet and I guess he felt the show wasn't quite gay enough yet.
> —David Greenwalt

"You always have to leave them wanting more," laughs Whedon. "What's a great show without a few cliffhangers."

Angel entered its fourth season looking very strong with some fascinating plot lines developing. Angel is rescued from his watery tomb by a morally ambiguous Wesley. Cordelia returns without her memory and befriends Connor, who now seems to be something of a male vampire slayer. The sixth episode of the season, *Spin the Bottle*, is written and directed by Whedon.

Angel's strength in season four comes despite some serious challenges. At the end of season three, coproducer Greenwalt announced that he was leaving the show (he would continue to serve as a creative consultant). Greenwalt moved to Touchstone Television, where he serves as the show runner for the new ABC fall-season drama *Miracles*.

Greenwalt did not leave because of any issues with Joss or the show, but because he saw the opportunity as too good to pass up. "An unex-

Angel site visit

During January 2000, I had the opportunity, along with several other television critics, to visit the set of *Angel*. While we were there, we had a chance to talk to Joss and the cast as a group, and then we had private chats with each of them.

The thing that struck me when we first walked in was how big the soundstage was, but how tiny the actual set containing Angel's living quarters. His bedroom and kitchen were so small that I can't imagine how they were able to film in there.

Now remember, this was the first season, before they blew everything up and moved to the big beautiful hotel.

Think a small New York apartment, maybe in Hell's Kitchen. Everything on the set was grimy and made to look dirty and old. The kitchen looked like any you might find in a small apartment. But there was one big difference. The refrigerator didn't work, but there was a nice supply of blood inside. The blood wasn't real, we were later told. But the fridge had one funky smell.

Those early episodes of *Angel* had a dark and gritty look, and the sets were exactly as you see them on screen. "You get used to it after a while," Carpenter told me during a private chat. "I'm one who likes things neat and tidy. There's a bit of Martha Stewart in me, but even I got used to it eventually. But it may have made me even a little more obsessive about keeping my home clean," she laughs.

While we chatted, I watched Boreanaz as he showed off his digs. He didn't see them as small and dirty at all. It was as if he was at home, showing off a castle. He was so proud and happy to have us there. It was kind of sweet, actually.

Joss was the same way. When someone made a derogatory remark about Angel's digs, the creator had a quick comeback. "Well, he is a vampire," Joss laughed. "What do you expect? He needs some place to sleep during the day and he has a fridge full of blood. What more does a vampire need?"

"Isn't he cute?" Carpenter said as we moved away from the group for our chat. "He's like a proud father," she said of Joss. "That's the great thing about being on this show; he and David are so into every detail. The sets and the characters, they care about everything. Now if I could just get them interested in my wardrobe," she laughed.

116

Joss concedes that Cordelia's wardrobe has not been a high priority. "She's the only girl around, and I guess we weren't paying much attention to the clothes she wears," he said. "We heard from a lot of women who watched her on *Buffy* and liked that she had all these cool clothes. Now she's on *Angel* and she wears jeans all the time. The truth is the character sort of hit rock bottom and doesn't have a lot of money for clothes. She's also been out in the field a lot more, fighting the bad guys, and she can't do that in high heels and dresses. I can't believe I'm the one talking to you about wardrobe," he laughs. "Look at me, I'm the last one to talk to anyone about the right clothes to wear."

One thing he did take offense at was the criticism that, when she wasn't wearing jeans, Cordelia's clothing was skimpy at best. When she was an actress trying to make it in Hollywood, there were a few low-cut dresses and bikinis on the show.

"If it involved the story for some reason, then we might have to do something like that, but it doesn't happen often," says Whedon. "We are more likely to make the guys dress in something ludicrous than we are Charisma."

"I don't mind getting to wear something sexy now and then," laughs the actress. "It reminds people that I'm not just one of the guys. Well, I am, but you know what I mean."

For the record, Joss himself was wearing his trademark T-shirt with a checkered shirt, jeans, and sneakers.

pected thing happened to me when I first read and then saw the pilot for *Miracles*, which is that I fell in love," says Greenwalt. "It's got everything—it asks the big questions about existence, it's got irony and danger and horror and hope, and these are all the things that I love.

"You know, I came from a show called *Profit*, but nobody in America saw it. But it made a splash, and I was lucky enough to work with Joss for six beautiful years. And, in fact, my contract was up at Fox. I took myself to the beach and watched the ocean. I said, 'You know, I think I'd like to be on my own.' And it wasn't fun to leave Joss and not work so intimately with him anymore, but for me it was like, this is a once-in-a-lifetime opportunity, and I want to be a part of this show. It's so good. . . . And it seems like a natural next step forward for me as well."

Whedon bears no ill will. "It's a good move for him," says Joss. "He's still gonna consult for *Angel*, so that's good for me, but it's killing me. I'm losing a great writer, a great producer, a great director, and a guy without whom I have yet to make an hour of TV. He's the real deal, and there aren't that many of those."

Whedon brought in David Simkins (*Roswell, Freaky Links*) as replacement show runner. This was an unusual move for Joss, as almost all of his senior staff grew up with *Buffy* and *Angel* and were part of this world long before they took on executive responsibilities. Joss acknowledged the challenges Simkins would face. "David [Simkins] is finding his feet. But you know you don't just walk into a show that someone else has created and instantly know the game. But he's aware of that and we are working with him. He's very smart and story-savvy, and he's an experienced producer."

But Simkins didn't work out and left after a few months. Executive producer Tim Minear expressed some sympathy for the difficulties Simkins had joining the *Angel* team. "It was an incredibly difficult situation to walk into . . . he was thrown into the deep end of the pool without any lifeguards, and so, because we didn't have the time to really get in there and break him in, just everybody decided that it wasn't going to work . . . But I didn't envy David Simkins being put into the middle of that situation, because it's difficult."

Minear insisted the show would not be hurt by Simkin's departure. "It's a machine that's running and in place, but at the end of the day, the season arcs and the stories are going to have to be broken by Joss and me and the staff, just like they have been since the beginning of the year, so it's not all that different, in that sense."

With Simkins gone, leadership of the show fell to Whedon and Minear, and Angel experienced one of its most successful seasons in history. That machine Minear referred to ran better than it had in years, even though its producers were more than a little busy with other projects.

New Worlds

7

"My big dream for Batman 3 was
that they would do a Dark Knight, and Superman
would come down and be a government stooge . . .
that was my dream."

—Joss Whedon

From *Buffy*'s launch in 1997 to the present day, *Buffy* and *Angel* clearly dominated Joss's time and energies. Nevertheless, Joss was also involved in countless other projects, from the *Fray* comics to planning new television series, from writing a song for Anthony Head's album to overseeing Mutant Enemy, his production company.

Joss had been playing with the idea of doing a comic for some time before deciding to launch *Fray* in 2001. He wanted a project that related to the world of *Buffy* and *Angel* without being part of it. So he developed the idea of *Fray*, a slayer from a world hundreds of years after *Buffy*'s.

Perhaps the greatest appeal of the comics for Joss was the opportunity to operate without limitations. "The great thing about comic books is you can do whatever you want as far as the story goes. There are no real limitations to what you can create, except that you have a small amount of space to do it in. I can have flying cars and huge skyscrapers and whatever I want visually and you just can't always afford to do that in film."

Joss has been reading comic books his entire life and has a great respect for them. There was the *Spider-Man*, *Warlock*, and *X-Men* in the early days. He continues to be a fan of *Daredevil* and reads *The Preacher* and *Sin City*.

Fray, looking very slayer-like.

As he has about most things, Joss has strong feelings about the comics that are being written today. Joss complains, ". . . I miss good old storytelling. And you know what else I miss? Superpowers. Why is it now that everybody's like 'I can reverse the polarity of your ions!' Like in one big flash everybody's Doctor Strange. I like the guys that can stick to walls and change into sand and stuff. I don't understand anything anymore. And all the girls are wearing nothing, and they all look like they have implants. Well, I sound like a very old man, and a cranky one, but it's true."

Whedon was determined that *Fray* would be written with the same quality standards as *Buffy* or *Angel*. He didn't want to do anything halfway and he took his time developing the stories and working with artist Karl Moline. Originally, he had thought he would do two or three books, but as the story began to grow, Joss couldn't give it up. In the end, *Fray* became an eight-part story (not yet completed as of this writing).

Stylistically, *Fray* looks something like *Blade Runner* or *The Fifth Element*. The buildings

And all the girls are wearing nothing, and they all look like they have implants. Well, I sound like a very old man, and a cranky one, but it's true. —Joss are stacked far into the sky and there are cars flying around Manhattan. There are the extremely wealthy and the incredibly poor and downtrodden. The radiation in the air and water has resulted in a world with both diseased humans and mutants, who live together.

Fray centers around the world of a reluctant slayer, Melaka Fray. In some ways, she's like Buffy, but with notable differences. Melaka is older when she finds out she is a slayer, and unlike Buffy, she is a thief, part of the underworld and without much sense of social responsibility.

For several hundred years there's been no need for a slayer, because magic, vampires, and demons no longer existed. Melaka and Erin, her sister, had difficult childhoods. Erin is a police officer, which naturally leads to conflict with Melaka. When Melaka discovers she's supposed to slay vampires, she wants nothing to do with it. If she can't make any money at it, she doesn't see the point.

In the second book, Melaka begins to sense her powers and realizes that she really is different from most people. While still reluctant, she begins to accept her responsibilities as a super heroine.

Unlike *Buffy* and *Angel*, *Fray* is more an adventure story than one about horror. That's something Joss did on purpose. There is a touch of gruesome horror now and then, but for the most part it's about Melaka dealing with her personal demons while reaching for a higher purpose. The reluctant superheroine must constantly deal with creatures that are beyond anything she could have ever imagined.

Whedon describes how the creation of a comic compares to television. "It's similar in that you're looking for the big moments, you're looking for the big emotions, and you're constantly saying 'these guys are overacting.' It's different in the sense that you have to choose a still picture that will convey what usually you would have movement to convey. When you're taking off in the air or landing, which one is the one you need to show? How much do [you] need to convey visually? How much can you do in one panel? That's different and pretty exciting, just because it's new."

Like most things Joss is involved with, *Fray* is successful. From the moment of its launch, the comic flew off the shelves. The first issue of the comic book sold out of its first printing of twenty-six thousand copies less than two weeks after it had been released. The success of the series forced Dark Horse Comics to publish an additional ten thousand copies per issue for the remainder of the series.

"*Fray* really clicks along, and it is, I think, everything you'd get out of a movie if Joss had an unlimited budget and all the time in the world," says Scott Allie, the editor of the series, in an interview on darkhorse.com. "The artists are really kicking ass. When Joss saw the final, lettered and colored pages for the first issue he really flipped—like a kid in a candy store who'd suddenly found he owned the joint. Dark Horse is just plain dumb-lucky to have him. I'd put Joss up against any comics writer, with the exception of Alan Moore."

> When Joss saw the final, lettered and colored pages for the first issue he really flipped—like a kid in a candy store who'd suddenly found he owned the joint. —Scott Allie

Whedon was as surprised as anyone at the success of the series. "Well, I of course wanted the comic to become a cult hit, but you never expect these things," says Whedon. "It's been very exciting to create this alternate universe for a slayer, and have people be so accepting. I'm working with some of the best in the business and that has a great deal to do with the success. But yes, I'd say I'm surprised about what's happened."

Joss has said that he's open to the idea of a *Fray* television series. "It would be very expensive, on account of all the flying cars and whatnot," Whedon said. "But I kept the option open to develop it for other media."

Whedon has also found time to develop three new television series—*Ripper*, *Buffy the Animated Series,* and *Firefly* (*Firefly* is discussed in the next chapter).

Ripper takes place in England and revolves around *Buffy*'s Giles. Anthony Head will star and the show, if green-lighted, will air on BBC. Joss describes *Ripper* as follows: "He's a very lonely character who has had his life tied up in this one woman, and then he has to come home and get over that. He had to find his life again. It's a mystery, but it's a very quiet and adult show. His family, dead and alive, are a big part of it. There are monsters who sort of represent what is wrong with humanity, but it isn't the frenetic scary kinds of monsters we see in *Buffy*. It's a mystery show with some horror aspects. We have a lot of ghosts in mind."

Joss promotes his *Fray* comics.

Whedon's tight schedule has delayed the show, but he remains committed to it. "There will come a day, soon I hope, when I can take the time to go over there and get it done," says Whedon. "Once I get there it won't take long. I know exactly what it is I need to do. I know how England itself will be a character in the show. There is so much to play off there and it is something, again, that I've always wanted to do. The character will be perfect for Anthony."

Anthony Head remains confident as well. "It will happen," he says. "Joss really wants to do it. Jane Espenson has already written scripts. He's been busy prepping [for *Firefly*] and it's going to take quite a workload. That suits me, because I've got a lot on my plate at the moment. Maybe some time in 2003 or 2004, maybe something will happen."

Enterprise visit with Joss

There was a party on the Paramount lot for all of the UPN shows. Joss and several members of the *Buffy* gang were there. It was a simple meet-and-greet where you chat a little and then eat and drink a lot.

Joss had both of his hands bandaged after an incident with limes, chicken, and some sunlight. The limes and sunshine had created a chemical reaction that burned his hands. It looked painful, but he was more embarrassed than anything. "Nothing more than my own stupidity," he said of the bandages.

The big draw for the party was a chance to see the sets of the UPN series *The Enterprise*. At the time none of us knew that Joss was working on his own space series, but he was like a kid on the set. At first I thought he might make fun, but there was nothing but joy on his face as we waited to go through the iron gates and into the first set.

I was in Joss's tour group. He listened carefully as different crewmembers explained the working parts of the sets. The first stop was the engine room and the main cabin of the ship. Joss played with the dials and sat in the captain's chair. He checked out every inch before we moved to the next set. I was busy making notes for a story I was working on, but it was hard to miss Joss as he turned all the knobs and pushed the buttons on the computers.

His cohort Marti Noxon was there right along with him. He turned to her a few times and said, "Man, we need one of these." At the time I had no idea what was going on in that mind of his, but it wasn't long after that party that the announcement was made about the pilot for *Firefly*. While it's been mentioned that *Firefly* is the anti-*Star Trek*, I'm not sure Joss sees it that way. He seemed to have a great deal of respect for the *Star Trek* legacy and, while he had fun, he was almost reverential about the whole thing.

Almost a year later, when I visited the *Firefly* set, Joss promised that he had not been trying to get ideas from *The Enterprise* visit. "I was curious and thought it would be fun to check it out, but I wasn't really looking for ideas for our show. I did get some ideas of what I didn't want to do. We weren't going to have the big swinging captain's chair because that had been done. But I know that no matter how much I say I wasn't on some kind of mission, people aren't going to believe me. I just thought it would be fun."

There's a childlike fascination Joss has with the world, and at the same time there is a worldly view of what is taking place. It's that dichotomy that makes him so interesting.

Joss shows us his damaged hands, caused by some combination of lime juice and sun.

The animated television series version of *Buffy* was also in planning for a long time. Whedon initially brought in famed comic-book artist Jeph Loeb to head up development.

Loeb was very enthusiastic about the project. "I've never met anybody who is responsible for so much and yet so generous with his time," says the *Superman* and *Batman* illustrator. "It's his sandbox but he'll invite anybody in to play. He's the first one to say, 'Bring it on.'" As for the cartoon's content, Loeb says, "We'll be dealing with the first season of *Buffy*. It was a short season, so Joss didn't get a chance to tell a lot of stories. Buffy will get her driver's license. She and Willow will have their first baby-sitting job." The show will also be written by the live action series' scribes and drawn by animators Loeb describes as "the best in the business."

> It's his sandbox but he'll invite anybody in to play. He's the first one to say, 'Bring it on.' —Jeph Loeb

Whedon is also clearly excited. "I've seen preliminary artwork and I'm just in love with it," says Whedon. "And, with the exception of Sarah, I believe that everyone is doing their own voices. There's zero money to be made. They're just like, 'Ooh, I get to be animated? That sounds like fun.'"

The series would be based on *Buffy*'s first season, with *Angel* still around, Willow still straight and in love with Xander, and with Xander still hot for Buffy. The series is intended to have the same quality and intensity of the original, but with solidly G-rated plots and dialogue.

But since the series had been continually delayed, by June 2002, when it was finally green-lighted, Loeb had to leave for another opportunity. Nevertheless, it is still hoped the series will go forward one day, with the writing duties being split between several writers on the show, including Joss, Doug Petrie, and Jane Espenson.

"When I was first brought in to interview, I was brought in to interview for the animated show," Petrie told BBC.com. "I was shown rough sketches of the characters and some of the sets. I loved what I saw, I was dying to work on the show and I was hoping once I was hired on the live action (series), I would still get a chance to work on it.

"It's going to be an amazing show. It's funny, exciting; it's all the huge

Joss yucks it up with Michelle Trachtenberg and Alyson Hannigan.

gigantic action that we can't do in a live show—so the sky's the limit. There are a lot of ideas that they've had in the past five seasons, that were great ideas but they just couldn't do, budget-wise. So we get to do all those cool high school stories that we couldn't tell back in high school. Plus it's the return to the classic *Buffy*, the way it all started, with all the teenagers and high jinks. It's going to be absolutely amazing."

"It does take a long time to put these things together," says Whedon. "I wanted to make sure that we had the right people and compelling stories. Yes, it's a cartoon, but that doesn't mean it can't be a good cartoon. If we are going to do it, I want it done right."

It's clear that Whedon's eclectic mix of projects will continue to grow in scale and variety. In April of 2002, Whedon hired Chris Buchanan as president of his production company, Mutant Enemy. In addition to overseeing Whedon's various television projects, Mutant Enemy will explore production of music and movies as well.

The success of *Buffy* and *Angel,* and his joy at producing them, stand in sharp contrast to Joss's frustration and disappointment at what he calls his "crappy film career." But the movie siren still calls to Whedon.

Whedon has written two scripts that have yet to be filmed. The first script, titled *Suspension*, was written early in his career. He unabashedly calls it "*Die Hard* on a Bridge." The most fun for Joss was figuring out "how many unbelievable things can happen on a bridge?"

"In *Suspension,* terrorists take over the George Washington Bridge," Joss tells. "Interestingly enough, I wrote it thinking, 'Okay, I've got the George Washington Bridge, and it's like *Die Hard*, so maybe I can sell it.' What I love about *Suspension* is that the lead character, Harry Monk, has just come out of prison. He's from New York and has been imprisoned in New Jersey for fifteen years and just wants to get to New York. That, right away, felt like the perfect thing for somebody who did not want to be on this bridge; somebody who just desperately wants to get back to New York. Then it's the whole redemption thing, because he was in jail for shooting a cop, so that when he hooks up with other policemen, they hate him; they don't trust him and he has to earn their trust. It's a redemption-through-violence story, which I like a lot."

> It's a redemption-through-violence story, which I like a lot. —Joss

The second script, *Afterlife*, is classic science fiction. It's about a scientist, Daniel Hoffstettor, who is slowly dying from a fatal disease. He and his wife, Laura, are trying to make the best of his last days, but the knowledge of his impending death hangs over their lives.

Then Daniel dies and (no surprise for Whedon fans) . . . wakes up! A government agency named Tank has transferred his brain into a virile young body. Daniel was given a second chance at life and the opportunity to continue his research. But Daniel wants more. He wants to see his wife again. So Daniel escapes but he soon finds that he is in the body of an executed serial killer. His face is infamous, and soon both Tank and the police are hunting him.

Even worse, the personality of Jamie Snow, the serial killer, is beginning to emerge and he must battle it to retain control of his body. He ultimately finds his wife but then must confront the forces chasing him.

The movie may be produced one day, so I won't reveal the ending. But according to screenwritersutopia.com, "Afterlife's finale is absolutely showstopping in its blindsided punch. Joss wraps all the threads in his hand and thrusts us toward a big, exciting, passionately zealous, sharp ending.

"Afterlife is a great Hollywood action-thriller with a grinning plot that seems so simple on paper but takes a grand master to craft into something that stays off the road of hokum. With equally large dollops of fantasy and reality, Joss is able to walk the center ground—and strike the heart of impermanent movie heat."

Joss also got involved with *X-Men*, doing a rewrite which was then almost entirely rejected. "I just felt there was some weak characterization," he said of the script he saw. "Long stretches with no forward momentum in the plot. And more importantly, there was no Danger Room [a staple of the *X-Men* comics]. So I put in a big Danger Room, I tried to keep it, you know, cheap. But they threw all that out. I was so excited about writing it. It was so much fun. I felt very passionate about it, which was probably a terrible mistake.

> I felt very passionate about it, which was probably a terrible mistake. —Joss

"I can't tell you how excited I was to write that film. They said, 'Hey you want to do this?' and I jumped at it. Who wouldn't? I love comic books and at that point no one had made a great movie from one. This was my chance to really make my mark, and then they trashed the whole thing. I think one line of what I had written was left in the film. It could have been so much better if they had let me do what I wanted with that one."

Like Charlie Brown running at the football, Joss again ran at the movies, only to fall flat on his back. "It's like, 'How many signs do I need?' Every time I do the same thing. *Alien Resurrection* happens and I go, 'Never again, I'll stay in TV where I'm happy.' Then the *X-Men* thing comes up and I say, 'That could be so cool.' So I dive in and they don't give a flying [expletive] what I think is cool. It's like I forget what a writer is in the movies, which is nothing. It's entirely true. My whole movie career has been a cautionary tale."

Halle Berry delivers one of the few Joss lines left in X-Men. "Do you know what happens when a toad is hit by lightning? The same as anything else.

firefly 8

"Fox came to Joss and said, do you
have any sort of uplifting, homegrown stuff that's
patriotic, and he said, 'I have [a] show about
depression in deep space.' And they said 'OK, we'll
have that . . .'"

—Anthony Head

"It's about the search for meaning . . . and did I
mention there's a whore?"

—Joss Whedon

Joss entered the 2002/2003 television season with a full plate. *Buffy* was in its seventh and final season, and Joss was determined to see it to a brilliant conclusion. *Angel*, just hitting its stride, faced the loss of both David Greenwalt and David Simkins. But despite these responsibilities, Joss's most important project was *Firefly*. Heavily promoted and launched on a major network, (Fox, by some measures, is one of the top-rated networks) *Firefly* was a high-profile new series. Unlike *Buffy*, *Firefly* would not have the luxury of operating in relative obscurity as it slowly develops its audience.

Joss was well aware of *Firefly*'s importance and he felt the pressure. "We aren't flying under the radar any more, I'll tell you that," Joss explains. "And that's a different feeling. I miss it [flying under the radar]. It's more pressure, but ultimately, developing a series is always complicated. *Firefly* is no exception, but neither were *Buffy* or *Angel*. It's a miserable process. More miserable than it should be. The fact is I have three shows now that I adore and are exactly as I had hoped they might be and more. So, ultimately the process must work."

Set five hundred years in the future, the hour-long drama takes place on a small transport spaceship named *Serenity*. *Serenity* is a Firefly-class spaceship (the ship lights up in the back and vaguely resembles a firefly). There has been an interstellar civil war, and the show focuses on the rough-and-ready crew of *Serenity*. The crewmembers are willing to take any job, legal or not, to stay afloat and make money. They are the cowboys of the Western frontier of the future. They seek adventure and, occasionally, try to find a purpose in a difficult world.

The idea for the show came about "three years ago, when I was reading *The Killer Angels*, the book on Gettysburg," says Whedon. "I just got obsessed. I'd always wanted to do a science-fiction show and I got obsessed with sort of the minutiae of life way back when—that early life, frontier kind of thing, when things were not so convenient as they are now. And I wanted to do a show in the future that really had that sense of history. The idea that it never stops, that we don't solve all our problems and have impeccably clean spaceships in the future; that we're all exactly the way we are now and were a hundred years ago . . . I got to thinking about what might have happened after the war, and then sort of ran with that into the future.

"The people on the ship are struggling to put meaning to their lives and find hope in a very dark time," continues Whedon. "They don't have easy lives by any means, but they make the most of what they have. I think great westerns aren't good guy/bad guy. And I think sometimes they're bad guy/worse guy. . . ."

> I think great westerns aren't good guy/bad guy. And I think sometimes they're bad guy/worse guy . . . —Joss

With *Star Trek* the prototypical starship series, Whedon was determined to do something different and unexpected. There are no aliens on *Firefly*, but Joss promises people "more frightening than any alien." And there are no strange planets. Remembering his budget frustration on *Buffy*, and knowing where he would have to shoot the show, he decided to make the most of what he had.

"Another part of the whole frontier thing was knowing that I was going to be shooting in Southern California, and that if we tried to build weird space worlds every week, . . . we won't be going back to Earth. But every planet is Earth. That's the one giant technological advancement that we luckily made," he says, tongue-in-cheek. "They found a galaxy with a bunch of planets, a bunch of moons, and were able to terraform all of them, so that you know there are no planets that look very bizarre. They've all been turned into little wannabe Earths."

While *Buffy* and *Angel* rely heavily on metaphors, Whedon wanted to take *Firefly* in a different direction. "*Buffy* bigger than life—*Firefly* actual size. And I think that's the important thing . . . You know, it's a different thing in the sense that I actually built *Buffy* to be a cult figure . . . an iconic figure that I wanted to devise. This is a very different show," he says of *Firefly*. "I believe it has the same kind of heart, and ultimately can have the same kind of following. But it's not about creating an icon. It's really about doing the opposite.

"The thing I love about this show is that they're not superheroes," he says. "They're not bigger than life. They're not, you know, fighting monsters and all that stuff. They go through the same struggles; they have the same problems and drama, and of course, action and all that stuff. But it's really about people who are just people. It's about the group. It's about life on this ship. It's *Stagecoach* [the classic John Wayne movie directed by John Ford].

"So it's not—you know, you don't go in there thinking, 'How can I make a cult show?' You go in there thinking what is the most compelling thing to me right now? And to me right now—what it was then was the adolescent metaphor, what it is now is really getting a chance to look at life from a lot of different points of view. That's why we have nine regulars."

> I believe it has the same kind of heart, and ultimately can have the same kind of following. But it's not about creating an icon. It's really about doing the opposite. —Joss

Firefly set visit

In July 2002, I had a chance to visit the sets for *Firefly* on the 20th Century-Fox lot and I discovered that Joss was right. There was very little his spaceship and the sets within had in common with what we had seen in television and film before. As you walk into the door of the first *Firefly* set, the enormity of it is overwhelming. Two huge bulbous thrusters poke out from each side of the two-story ship, and the cargo-bay door lies open like a giant mouth. The actual cargo area is filled with boxes, trunks, and giant barrels that are made of various types of colored plastic. It's dirty and a little musty. There's lots of black and brown, and everything is in muted tones.

Chinese lettering marks the walls and cargo on the ship, evidence of China's power and influence in the years before the war. I could see where Inara's shuttle would normally be docked off to the right side of the ship.

Joss explained that while most of the spaceships we've seen on TV and film were clean and almost pristine, he wanted his to look like someone actually used it. The walls are a grungy gray, and overhead there are metal walkways that look well used. As you enter through the large cargo bay, there is a sliding metal door that you duck through and walk into a small lounge area. The eclectic and well-worn furniture looks like something you might find in a '60s bachelor pad mixed with stuff from your grandma's living room.

To the left is the infirmary, which is the cleanest-looking room on the set. The white-and-silver walls look very sterile. Metal tables, small computers, and a variety of bandages occupy the spotless counters.

Past the infirmary, I walked up a large ramp leading up to some of the travelers' quarters where the guests stay. It's a tight fit (think jail cell minus a few feet), and many of the scenes shot in the area can only be done with a handheld camera—this free form of shooting lends the show that stylized look Joss deemed appropriate for a space adventure. Though small, the room seems complete with a sink, bed, and places for clothing. This warmly decorated room feels more homey than the rest of the set. The oxygen mask lodged in the wall by the bed reminds you that this is the set of a spaceship and not a spare room in some suburban home.

Back out through the cargo bay, we walked across the street to a different soundstage to find a bright and cheerful galley, painted yellow with delicate leaf accents. A huge wooden table takes up much of the space with several different kinds of chairs. The eclectic hodge-podge mix of wood and plastic furniture somehow seems to work in the space. It feels very lived-in, like a big family kitchen. It certainly doesn't look like what you'd expect to find in the future; it's pretty low-tech.

A small hatch in the wall leads to Kaylee's home, the engine room. You definitely know that you're in a spaceship when you step into the mechanical gloom; what a striking contrast to the sunny galley! Kaylee's hammock is the only hint that someone actually lives here; everything has such a technical look. This is such a far cry from the look and feel of the *Buffy* and *Angel* sets I've visited. It's difficult to imagine that those worlds and this one were born of the same mind.

Though this particular set is 190 feet from the tail end to the nose and takes up a good portion of the soundstage, it was crowded with crew members, equipment, and props. After poking around the set a bit more, we ended our tour so that the busy crew could do their jobs away from the prying eyes of curious journalists.

In *Firefly*, Whedon again tries to break the rules in his depiction of what space looks and sounds like. In *Firefly*, he has taken every stereotype about space travel and reworked it into his own unique vision.

"It's largely influenced by westerns, but hopefully with a twist. But the thing about the West that people forget about is that it was full of immigrants. And that was another thing, every time people are colonizing or stealing a new area, they bring the old world with them. And in this case, every old world. And some of them have meshed, and some of them have, you know, stayed, and some of them have changed.

"Also a very heavy Asian strain, because in my vision of the future, you know, America and China have basically been the big powers, and the two ruling planets are basically those planets; they really are the Alliance. And that's why everyone speaks Chinese; there's Chinese writing everywhere. And it's just sort of been incorporated into American culture."

Whedon has gone so far as to create a dialect for the characters. Most of them come from different planets, but there is a specific 1900s sound with a bit of a twist. "English evolves constantly. I sort of took from a lot of older things, and in particular, westerns. Not just westerns, but, in particular, westerns. Plus making stuff up, because I don't speak too good, so I just have to lie. But the idea, you know, of the frontier, was so important to what makes the show, the idea of the western. That's what I wanted to draw on the most.

"You kind of feel your way through it. Like *Buffy* . . . People can bring their own thing to it. But there is a kind of rhythm to it that the writers are already starting to get down. But you just feel when it's wrong, when it's too much or when it's incoherent or when it doesn't flow. You just sort of make it up as you go."

Joss Whedon wrote the opening music. "The whole idea with the music, first of all, was to evoke to some extent the western feel. And also, you know, just to get away from, you know the bombast of space, space, and space! It's very much—it's just normal life. And I wanted to put something else in people's heads when they see spaceships. I didn't want the giant, orchestral, Jerry Goldsmith thing. Not that I don't love Jerry and all of that other stuff, but I just felt that it had become de rigueur. That like we expected to hear big explosions and hear great big orchestras every time we went into space. And for these people, space, you know, it's the wagon trail. It's not that big a deal. And that's what I want the audience to feel in that sense."

Whedon also wanted to try something that had never been done before. When his spaceships go to full power and we see the thrusters burn, there's no loud explosions. "We decided since there is no sound in space, and since most of it takes place, you know, where there will be sound, it just—it felt real, and it also helped sort of get rid of the space that we are used to seeing."

As noted earlier, *Firefly* does not feature aliens, just humans, good and bad. "I'm not going, 'No creatures, this is a western," says Joss. "I'm going, 'No creatures, this is reality.' That really is the mission statement. I wanted to stay away from the easy science-fiction fixes, the android, the clone, the alien, all the stuff that, for all I know, may be lurking around the corner, but I'm not expecting to see any time soon. You know, I wanted to go low-tech. It's not so much about being a western."

". . . It's just about life when it's hard. And for me, it's about the idea of people always being people, always having the same problems that they had, putting it in kind of an exotic setting, having a spaceship, getting

The cast of *Firefly*. Will they remain grounded?

to tell some adventure stories, because I do love science fiction, but not playing—again it gets you into that grandeur.

"And here's the thing I've never seen. What I'm looking for is people to go, 'These guys are me'; I feel that. I mean they're cooler and they dress better and they're taller," Joss laughs, "but they are. They're going through the same kind of struggles we are. They're trying to pay the rent; they're trying to buy gas; they're trying to get these things at the same time as, you know, with the gunfighting and all the stuff, and the chasing and the Reavers [debased humans who cannibalize their victims].

"But I really wanted to get that more than anything else, that feeling of reality, which is why so much of the show is handheld. I was like, I want to shoot this thing like it's *NYPD Blue*, like, you know, these are the mooks that we all know; they just happen to be future mooks.

". . . I believe we're the only sentient beings in the universe. And I believe that five hundred years from now, we will still be the only sentient beings around. And aliens, you know, that's something everybody else has done, is doing. I don't know a lot of the newer shows, but I know that there are a lot of shows out there, and they all share that kind of thing. And that's a great metaphor to play with.

"But it's not really what I'm interested in. I'm really interested in 'You are there,' in 'You are a part of this.' And I think aliens, no matter what, take you out of that. I also need to spend some time away from latex," he laughs.

Another way Joss differentiates *Firefly* from his other shows is by not throwing in a lot of pop culture. While there are some things from the twentieth century that find their way into the future, Whedon was determined to keep it simple. "The Beatles, I'm sorry that's Shakespeare," says Whedon. "So that survives. But, you know, Backstreet Boys, not so much. We'll make some references every now and then because we live in this time; it's a part of our nature. But it's not like *Buffy*, where it's just a pop-culture blender, and let's talk about everything. . . I want to maintain the reality of it. And the reality of it is most of the things that we think of as really important will have—myself included—will have disappeared into the dust long, long before these guys ever see the light of day.

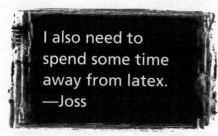

I also need to spend some time away from latex.
—Joss

"It's not like we've forgotten everything. We used up Earth. We colonized a new galaxy. We've made it all a bunch of little Earths, but we remember. I mean, we do have written records and all that stuff. And Betamax comes back," he laughs.

There is a great deal of violence in the show, but Whedon is careful to never be gratuitous with it. "The trick is, you know, always for there to be some meaning or consequence when—every time you draw a gun. That's why not everybody—a character—can or will," says Whedon. "The show having become a little more of an action show, there will be a slightly higher body count because of that. But the trick is never to get so cavalier with it that it has no meaning whatsoever.

"How we make decisions is basically about what feels right and natural, and what we need," says Whedon. "Now, the fact is we could have laser beams. The problem for me is that laser beams instantly feel safe to people. A laser beam can be set to stun. A laser beam makes a cool visual. And I wanted the violence in the show to feel violent. When Kaylee gets shot, I wanted a bullet wound. I wanted it to matter to us the way it matters to us now. And the idea that, yeah, they may have invented cool lasers, but not everybody can afford them, is sort of the premise on which we work.

"And sometimes, you know, we may get it wrong. But basically, the idea is whatever feels sort of natural and endemic is what works. But it has to ring true to us emotionally. And laser beams just were not there. And they take you to a science-fiction place that I feel has been covered too much," says Whedon.

In casting *Firefly*, Joss continued his tradition of taking risks on relative newcomers such as Brendon (Xander), Boreanaz (Angel), Acker (Fred), and Hallett (Lorne). None of the cast are big-name actors. Some, like Summer Glau, who plays River, have virtually no previous acting experience (Glau's television debut was in *Angel*'s "Waiting in the Wings" episode, which Joss says was her screen test for *Firefly*). "I only hire incredibly talented people with no experience," says Whedon, "so I don't have to do a lot of work. Believe me, I've hired a lot of people with a ton of experience who couldn't walk through a door . . . I just love finding these people who've done nothing."

The makeup of the characters and the development of them are a huge priority to Joss and his coproducer Tim Minear. No one is superfluous, and the intention was to reveal their hidden depths over time. "We have nine very specific voices, nine very specific characters," says Minear. "All of them have different points of view. I find this show much easier to write than *Angel*, because on that show all of the characters have the same agenda. Basically they are all trying to accomplish the same thing. We changed that a little bit by breaking off Wesley and starting to give other characters different points of view, but they still have the same vision.

> Believe me, I've hired a lot of people with a ton of experience who couldn't walk through a door . . . I just love finding these people who've done nothing. —Joss

"But when I was writing the big exposition scenes for this show, everyone had a point of view and everyone had an agenda. It was much easier to write. Instead of everyone saying, 'We all have the same goal, how are we going to accomplish it,' there was some argument about

SUE SCHNEIDER / MOONGLOW PHOTOS

Nathan Fillion plays Captain Malcom Reynolds, who took the role despite Joss having gone "Agent Smith on him."

what the goal was and what they should be doing. All of that became a dialogue and it just made it easier."

The lead character is Captain Malcolm (Mal) Reynolds, played by Nathan Fillion. Mal is an angry guy who fought on the losing side in the civil war. He does whatever it takes to make a quick buck, but he operates from a moral code, albeit a unique one.

For Fillion, taking on the role of Captain Reynolds was a terrific change from the bumbling oafs he had played in *Saving Private Ryan* and *Dracula 2000*. He wasn't at all sure he could pull it off, but he was willing to give it a try. "After I finished my sitcom with 20th Century-Fox, *Two Guys and a Girl,* they had given me a deal; [they were] kind enough to keep me around and look for a job for me. They set me up with a meeting with Joss Whedon, the genius who brought us *Buffy the Vampire Slayer*, and I walk into this office, and I'm thinking, 'Where's Joss?' And he's this guy in the corner with the scraggly beard and this crazy hair, talking like this, 'Oh it's going to be a great show,'" laughs Fillion.

> I walk into this office, and I'm thinking, 'Where's Joss?' And he's this guy in the corner with the scraggly beard and this crazy hair, talking like this, 'Oh it's going to be a great show.'
> —Nathan Fillion

"I did. I don't know why," laughs Joss about the strange voice he was doing during the meeting. "I went all Agent Smith on him."

"But we talked about this wonderful show," says Fillion. "I'd only read a treatment for the script, like a play-by-play; basically, what's going to happen. And I was in love with it. I said, I love this character. I love how dark he is. I love how he makes such hard decisions. I love what a tough-ass he is. I'm so NOT this guy," he laughs. "But he had me come in and audition anyway, and he gave me the part."

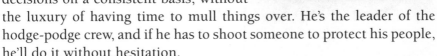

I went all Agent Smith on him. —Joss

Captain Reynolds must make tough decisions on a consistent basis, without the luxury of having time to mull things over. He's the leader of the hodge-podge crew, and if he has to shoot someone to protect his people, he'll do it without hesitation.

"That's another thing that interests me about Mal," says Whedon. "He's is very much 'I'm pure pragmatist,' but at the same time he will lay down his life for his crew, for these people. They are his family. He takes care of them. He, you know, he has that hardness, but with that hardness he doesn't really admit to himself how he feels about them most of the time."

Zoe (Gina Torres) served with Mal in the war and is also a mercenary, thief, and smuggler when necessary. She sticks with her friend through thick and thin and there's a lot of friendly chemistry between the two characters. Romance is not a possibility, since she's married to Wash (Alan Tudyk), who is the calm one in the bunch. And it's a good thing, because he's the pilot of the ship.

"I was thrilled that this was a woman who was clearly layered," says Torres. "And it wasn't just—she wasn't just a bad-

Gina Torres plays Zoe, Mal's second in command. Torres has also guest starred on *Alias*, and plays a role in the *Matrix* sequels.

Sean Maher plays Simon Tam, the Central Worlds doctor who sacrificed everything to save his sister.

ass. You know she has a relationship. She has a mission. She's righteous. She's great. And there's a lot of—there's a place to go with that. There are a lot of places to go with that."

Simon Tam (Sean Maher) is a wealthy doctor from the center of civilization. "Simon and his sister, River, are on the run from the Alliance because she was being experimented on and he discovered it," Minear says. "He rescued her from her torture and now they are on the run on this ship. I think Simon is a guy who came from a privileged background and who probably supported the unification of the planets. He was on the side of the government during this war, and now finds himself on this ship with these rebels. He couldn't have imagined himself here before, but he's got nowhere else to go."

Summer Glau plays psychic River Tam, Simon's sister. River is a genius of sorts, but she also suffers from government experiments gone awry. She usually says the wrong thing at the wrong time and has a way of creating chaos at inopportune times.

Adam Baldwin (not one of the brothers) portrays Jayne. "Jayne is sort of mercenary who signs on to make a living and this is just what he does," says Minear. "This guy is a straight-on mercenary and it's sometimes hard to figure just how far he will go to make some money. He's big and mean and loves to fight. If someone needs to be killed, Jayne is the go-to guy. Yet he does have a soft spot for Kaylee."

Jewel Staite plays Kaylee, the ship's mechanic. "She's a cheery, upbeat engine-room professional, she's the Scotty of the show," laughs Minear. "She's a happy girl who loves life and can fix just about anything. While her cheerful personality sometimes wears on the crew's nerves, there isn't a one of them who wouldn't lay their life on the line for her."

Inara (Morena Baccarin) is the "companion" on the ship, or, as Joss delicately put it, "She's the whore." She helps smooth relationships with any onboard guests and entertains them. She's dubbed "The Ambassador" for her easygoing ways, but she isn't to be taken lightly.

"Inara is very classy, you know she isn't what you think of when you think of a whore," says Baccarin. "Joss has written this wonderful, beautiful character, who brings the class and nurturing in the spaceship, which is really great. I get to do all of these super things, like know how to play instruments in bands and wear pretty dresses and be classical. It's wonderful."

Ron Glass plays Book the Shepherd. He's a traveling man who is out to see the universe and spread the good word. He's a nice guy, but isn't afraid to get his hands dirty if necessary.

Alan Tudyk plays Wash, Serenity's pilot, and Zoe's husband.

"He's clearly a man of letters, and a man of the Word, so to say, and he has a big heart," says Glass of the Shepherd. "He's really interested in people's humanity and people's advancement and their consciences and that kind of thing. At the same time I think he lived a lot of life before he became that person, and he has a lot to offer these other characters Joss has created.

"He's done an amazing job of pulling all of these different people together," says Glass. "Joss is like a present, he's like a gift as far as I'm concerned. He's so bright, creative, and inspiring, and he creates this ideal situation for actors to come in and do

> Joss is like a present, he's like a gift as far as I'm concerned.
> —Ron Glass

their thing. I'd never seen his other shows, but I consider it sheer luck that I ended up here. I had no idea what a blessing it would be."

The idea had come to Joss several years earlier, but when Fox called, he had to pull it all together incredibly fast.

The show itself met several challenges before and after the pilot was shot. After the advertisers met in May 2002, Fox wanted Joss to reshoot the pilot episode. They wanted more humor and action. There were also a few cast changes.

Adam Baldwin plays Jayne, who serves as both the muscle and the source of much of the humor in *Firefly*.

SUE SCHNEIDER / MOONGLOW PHOTOS

"Sometimes you do things on the business side that's not the best thing for the creative side," says Fox Entertainment president Gail Berman, "and when Joss came in and pitched his one-hour idea for a pilot, it was a very big show, and it would prove to be an expensive one. And we felt, corporately, that we might do better with it as a two-hour, be able to launch it as a feature internationally.

"So we asked him to expand to a two-hour and it went into a lot of back story, and when we saw the two-hour, as good as we thought it was, we felt there was a better way to launch this, with a more action-packed one-hour. And so we sat down with Joss and discussed it with him, and he too felt at that point that starting this thing in a more aggressive way would probably be a better way to start the series. And so we decided to push the two-hour to a special event in season, and then launch [with] the one-hour."

Whedon took the comments from the network in stride. "Like anything you do, there are always things you work out as you go along," says Whedon. "Your initial vision is always there but you have to make it work within the context of what you are doing, and within a budget.

Summer Glau plays disturbed psychic River Tam. Glau won the role after impressing Whedon in *Angel's* ballet episode, "Waiting in the Wings."

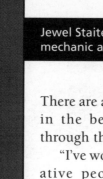

Jewel Staite plays Kaylee, the ship's mechanic and resident sweetheart.

There are always going to be changes in the beginning and as you go through the process. It never stops."

"I've worked with a lot of very creative people in my time," says Berman, "and I think Joss is as close to a genius as I know one to be. He has an incredibly keen understanding of storytelling in a way that I've rarely seen displayed elsewhere. He's so funny and smart, and I've worked with him as a colleague and producer, and I'm working with him now at the network. He's one of the great pleasures of my career."

"When I first read the script, I knew that he had something wonderful with *Firefly*, if they let him have the freedom to make it the way he wants too," says Professor Basinger. "See, that's where you run into trouble, is when the network wants to make this change or that. If they let Joss make his show, and trust him as the WB did with *Buffy*, then it is fantastic.

"With *Firefly* we talked about it being this group of people flying through space as a kind of a metaphor for plowing across the prairie. I was raised on the prairie and he asked me questions about what that was like. I told him about being surrounded by wide-open spaces. He [is] always thinking and questioning. It isn't just 'well, we will have guys with big foreheads on a spaceship.' It's not going to be like that. It's going to be something different."

> He has an incredibly keen understanding of storytelling in a way that I've rarely seen displayed elsewhere. —Gail Berman

Whedon is as much a fan of westerns as he is science fiction. He uses many of those early influences in his work and blends them together seamlessly. "I'm a huge John Ford fan. I'm a huge westerns' fan. Anthony Mann, particularly. The '70s westerns, Altman, you know they were a huge influence. The '70s, because they really stopped using the iconography that had become ossified and said 'What was it really like?' a bit more, and you really got that sense of life in things like *McCabe and Mrs. Miller, Ulzana's Raid,* and, actually, I'll probably get in huge trouble for mentioning this, *Heaven's Gate,*" he laughs.

"Life is hard out there," says Whedon of the world he has created in space. "I wanted to see that world I miss. You know, a world without the Internet and Pink Dot. A world where, you know, things have to be made from scratch, including decisions, ethics.

"You create a civilization when you go into space. You bring it with you. And how you do that is a really personal process, and to me, a fascinating one. And the harder things are, the more times your ethics and your moral structure are going to be tested. Plus, more adventure.

"And to me, you know, when I pitched the show, I said, 'This is about nine people looking into the blackness of space and seeing nine different things,'" says Whedon. "And that's really what I'm fascinated by, is how they all react to this.

"I think it's just more interesting than, you know, 'Because he's our client, dammit!' But that's me. I mean, a lot of people do that well. I can't do that well. 'I'll allow it, but you'd better be going somewhere with this,'" he laughs again. "I just feel like there's a group of people that aren't represented, in a way, the people who really are just living hand-to-mouth. . . that's what fascinates me."

Because *Firefly* is so different from *Buffy* in tone, not every *Buffy* fan has appreciated the series. But the quality of the series is strong, and, although there was some negative buzz surrounding the

Ron Glass plays Book the Shepherd, a spiritual man with a decidely worldly past.

Morena Baccarin plays the companion Inara, the most respectable member of the crew.

network maneuvering on the pilot, criticism has been fairly positive. In particular, critics have noted that in a field of very similar programs, *Firefly* is truly unique. *TV Guide* says "Bucking the timidity of a TV season lacking in originality, Fox's funky *Firefly* may be guilty of overcompensating. You don't get more offbeat that this . . . But once you get used to it, *Firefly* is very entertaining. The characters are cleverly conceived and the crisp writing balances action, tension and humor nicely."

Like *Buffy*, *Firefly* integrates multiple genres. *Bushwacked*, in which we first encounter the Reavers (or, at least, their handiwork) is genuinely scary, but with moments of great humor. While *Our Mrs Reynolds*, written and directed by Joss, is an almost pure comedy, hysterical, but with moments of great action.

From the beginning, *Firefly*'s ratings have been mediocre and its future in doubt. Despite the enthusiasm of fans and the encouragement of critics (*TV Guide* said "let's hope Fox exercises some patience. Cult followings aren't born overnight"), the show was given a fairly short time period to find its audience. Despite some encouraging sign, including the ordering of new episodes by Fox, by mid-December of 2002 it was clear that *Firefly*, technically on "hiatus," would not return. Joss acknowledged as much in his December posting:

Four AM. Can't sleep. Who'd have thought?

There's a couple of things I'd like to say. And a few things I really can't. First of all, I'm prouder of this show and the people I worked with on it than I can express in words, monkey noises, or hieroglyphics. I believe this has been some fairly great TV. And the experience of making it... I've had crew members who've been working for 20 years say they've never worked around such excitement, support and love. You walk on that set, you're transported. The cast: 9 count 'em 9 incredibly talented actors who are all decent, wonderful people. This phenomenon cannot be explained by science.

Second of all, don't think for a second that I have given up on this show. I think it has been mistreated shamefully, but the Fox network has indicated that they would not stand in the way (which they can) of my finding a new home for the show. That's no easy prospect. But I will do everything in my power, as always, to keep this bird in the air. Of course I'll post if there's any news.

But even if the show goes back up elsewhere, I'm going to lose a good portion of my crew. Production will halt, they'll need to find new jobs. You can't imagine how that feels. How much they brought to the table, how hard and well they worked. And their Christmas bonus is this. As much as the cast, the staff, and my not so secret lover Minear, I honor those guys, and hope to get them back on board.

So for now, I proudly take my place beside *Profit*, *The Ben Stiller Show*, *the Tick*, and *Action*. But I won't rest until I've found safe harbour (no, not the Gregory Harrison show) for this vessel.

I've got the time.

It ain't like I'm sleeping.

-joss

Joss the Mentor

9

"He brings along talent and, in a way, nurtures it. I've learned so much just by being around him."

—Marti Noxon

Whedon may have started life as a shy reclusive boy, but he has learned to work effectively with his writing team, cast, and crew. Whedon has developed into a skilled director, leader, and mentor, and one gets the impression that this transformation was quite deliberate. Just as he changed his name to Joss to launch his Hollywood career, Joss quite deliberately built the skills he needed to realize his vision. He taught himself to direct and, equally challenging, he taught himself to be the leader and a mentor for his cast and crew.

Joss has developed a low-key, self-effacing style of leadership. He isn't harsh and he doesn't scream, but he is very demanding and it's absolutely clear to everyone that he is totally in charge.

"He knows what needs to happen," says Greenwalt. "I've worked with him on *Buffy* and *Angel* and he is probably one of the most focused men I've ever met. At the same time he's just a guy doing something that he loves, and it's that joy he has that makes everybody want to be there. It's hard not to want to work with someone who is so passionate about everything that he does."

"We all spend more time on the set than we do at home," says Whedon, "so you have to

> I've worked with him on *Buffy* and *Angel* and he is probably one of the most focused men I've ever met. —David Greenwalt

create that dynamic where people feel like they are all working toward the same thing. When people enjoy what they're doing and have fun at the same time, they are going to do a better job."

> **He believes in people.**
> **—Marti Noxon**

"He believes in people," says Noxon. "His instincts are unbelievable. Is he a good boss? Yes, because he makes you work hard and at the same time you never realize just how hard you really are working. That's what is so great about him. He makes it fun to be a part of it. I don't mean sappy kind of ha-ha fun. But like you-are-working-on-something-important-and-it's-all-heading-in-the-right-direction kind of fun."

Whedon's executive producers make it sound like fun and games, but these shows take a lot of time to film. The hours are long, and the cast and crew have their cranky moments. There are also times when the stories fall off track and they must work quickly to get things back in order. Joss, for all his kindness, is unrelenting on issues of quality.

Whedon invests a great deal of time in mentoring and developing his staff. Many of the people who work with him in high-level positions started as assistants or interns. He has a way of teaching and pushing without being obnoxious about it.

"Look at him," says Basinger. "He's a young guy in this business and he's incredibly generous and nurturing. He gets so excited when someone else has an idea and does something great. He definitely builds up talent. His first assistant that he hired was one of my students. He has moved on and now writes for *Dawson's Creek*. Joss spent a lot of time reading his work and helping him. You don't see that much in Hollywood and you certainly don't see it in the young people who are still making their way."

Whedon often returns to his alma mater to encourage the new film students in their work. "I taught my musicals class in the fall [of 2001]," Basinger continues. "He was very excited I was doing it because he was doing *Buffy the Musical*. So we kept talking about it on the phone and going over stuff. I always feel it's not good to ask favors. Finally he called me and he asked, so how is your class doing? I said, 'Oh they are great. They love the films and we are really into this.' He asked, 'Are they going to watch *Buffy the Musical*?' And I told him of course they were, I was giving it as an assignment.

Joss with *Buffy* executive producer Marti Noxon, who he calls, "one of great brains and beauty" (and she's a pretty good singer as well).

"And then a while later, he called back and asked if I thought the students might like it if he came by. I laughed and said, 'Are you kidding?' I said, 'I didn't feel I should ask you.' He's in the middle of his season working his butt off and I'm going to ask him to fly back to Middletown to ask him to talk to my musicals class. But he volunteered. He came and he showed *Buffy* and they went wild for it. He talked about what he learned. He said, 'Everything I know about musicals I learned in this room,' which of course isn't true. He learned plenty more somewhere else. I didn't teach him to compose music.

"The thing is that it was great for my class because it made them feel like if he could do it, maybe they could. He's very generous in that regard. He's wonderful to them. He listens to them and answers questions. He takes them seriously and he encourages them. And best of all he hires them. He's hired a lot of our graduates to work for him. Right outside his door, one to the left and one to the right, sit two Wesleyan film majors. He's taken interns and been great about that."

> The thing is that it was great for my class because it made them feel like if he could do it, maybe they could. He's very generous in that regard.
> —Jeanine Basinger

It is difficult to find anyone who has worked with Joss, past or present, who has anything bad to say about the man. He inspires loyalty in his casts and crews, and in the process teaches his generosity to others.

"He really gave me a chance when no one else would," says Noxon. "He pushes you to be better than you ever thought you could be. He's the one who pushed me into directing, and it was something I was very afraid of at the time. He does that, though, for everyone. There isn't a person here who isn't a hundred times better than when she or he came to the show. And that comes from Joss. He brings along talent and in a way nurtures it. I've learned so much just by being around him. Sort of by osmosis."

Joss the Genius

One of the odder things about researching Joss Whedon is how often the word "genius" comes up. After all, we're talking about a television writer, not a Nobel Prize winner. Is Joss Whedon a genius? Here's what some of his colleagues had to say:

"I can't tell you the thoughts that went through my brain when the word 'musical' came up, I couldn't imagine how it would work, which is why Joss is the one writing it. And you can't tell him no. He's lovable, kind, funny, but you don't tell him no. So we made a musical, and we actually had a lot of fun doing it. To be honest, I'm sure there were times when Joss wasn't sure he could pull it off, but he did it. That's the genius of Joss. . . .

"There are times when I've gone to him and I didn't understand why we were doing certain things and he explains it in such a way that it all makes sense. You just have to trust in that genius."

—Sarah Michelle Gellar

"Is there a word beyond 'genius'? It is crazy. I know he doesn't sleep and he certainly doesn't have time to eat. Why is that man alive? He has three shows on air and makes phenomenal television. He's an incredible storyteller, writer, and director. I hope there is something very wrong with him, because he is way too talented."

—Alexis Denisof

"Then meeting Joss . . . he's one of the most amazing people I've ever met in my life. He's a genius."

—Sean Maher

"That's the great thing about working with Joss, he's like an actor's dream. He's great with actors and he's really into listening and collaborating. He's very intelligent, articulate, and kind. People call him a genius, but I think it's a huge understatement."

—Morena Baccarin

Joss shares an affectionate moment with Alexis Denisof.

"I couldn't tell as the season went on, and I feel really strongly about this, if I was the one in control of the character. I thought I had control of him on my own. The reason Joss is brilliant is that I think he was manipulating me so well that he made me feel like I was in control and in reality it was him the whole time."

—Adam Busch

"There's not a question about [whether Joss is a genius]. I don't know of anyone who has met him that doesn't think he is amazing."

—Amy Acker

"I loved Joss Whedon. He's so smart and creative. He made one of the scariest things I've ever seen in my life. Did you see the episode where the guys are floating down the street, 'Hush'? I watched it in my own living room and it scared the hell out of me. I felt like a little kid again. I'd never seen that before. These guys were chilling.

"Then he did that musical, which was just amazing. I just think guys like him are just a breed of their own. They are so far ahead of the times and just have incredible creative capacity."

—John Ritter

"Joss is a genius and given half a chance to show what he could do I knew some kind of magic would happen."

—Gail Berman

"You don't get much more real talent than Joss Whedon."

—Seth Green

"It was the most wonderful experience of all time. It's been something I've been looking forward to from the first moment we were doing the presentation for the pilot and Joss and I and Sarah Michelle were talking about loves, and we all said how much we love musicals. I said, 'You love musicals too,' and he said, 'Yeah.' And I said, but I do musicals, and we said well we must do one together. Every year I'd ask him if we were going to do it this year, and he'd say, 'No, no,' because we don't want it to look like we are doing it because we can't do anything else. Then he had this idea of how to take simple story lines and he took that and turned it into pure genius."

–Anthony Head

The Real Joss

10

"I don't want to create responsible shows with lawyers in them. I want to invade people's dreams."

–Joss Whedon

Joss Whedon's talents as a writer, director, and producer are undeniable, but talent is only part of the picture. Behind Joss's low-key, self-deprecating exterior lies a man with an incredible intensity and drive. But Joss's ambition doesn't lie in the conventional mode. Growing up, Joss found the world to be a scary, unfriendly place. He found solace in the world of the imagination. Often the comfort of television, movies, music, and comics were all that sustained him. This has become his life's work–creating worlds of meaning, passion, and hope in an unfriendly and meaningless world.

Whedon has become a wealthy man, but he isn't driven by money. He's become successful, but success in the conventional sense doesn't motivate him. Joss is first and foremost a fan working for his fans, and for him success is about getting under the skin of his fans. "The most obsessive, nerd fans of this show are me and my writing staff," he says. "I can stump anybody on any episode. I've said this before, but it is how I feel and I know no other way to say it exactly: I would rather have a hundred people who *need* to see this show than a thousand people who *like* to see this show."

> I would rather have a hundred people who *need* to see this show than a thousand people who *like* to see this show. —Joss

Whedon describes himself as a "bitter atheist" who finds meaning only in his creations. "I'm a scary, depressive fellow. There's no meaning to life.

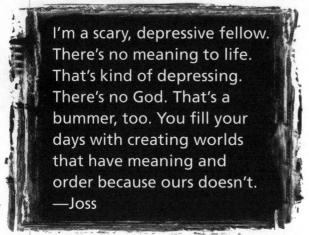

I'm a scary, depressive fellow. There's no meaning to life. That's kind of depressing. There's no God. That's a bummer, too. You fill your days with creating worlds that have meaning and order because ours doesn't.
—Joss

That's kind of depressing. There's no God. That's a bummer, too. You fill your days with creating worlds that have meaning and order because ours doesn't. And so, yeah, I'd say the fact that I'm a pretty depressive fellow also has to do with my ambition, staving off the inevitable."

Joss's need to write and create new worlds seems to extend beyond the normal creative drive; it's what keeps him going. "You know, I always get cranky when I'm not writing," Joss admits. "I'll be mad and I don't know why. I just feel like I'm angry with everybody, and I hate everything, and life is a sham. Then I'll realize I haven't written anything. And rewriting doesn't count. It has to be an original script."

This explains Whedon's intense frustration with what many would have considered a very successful screenwriting career. It wasn't enough to be writing and contributing. Joss is a world-builder and he has to be creating worlds that he controls, that have meaning for him. Television was the only way he could achieve this.

"It makes perfect sense to me [to work in TV as opposed to films] but it definitely surprises most people," Joss insists. "Why are the best writers in TV? Because they can control their product; they're given something resembling respect and they see what they create come up on the screen not only the way they want it, but also within a few months as opposed to–like–four years . . . I love movies and want to make more movies, but if the idea is to tell the story, then this is the best way to do that.

"Although I've been treated well by good people a lot of the time," he reflected, "I have the usual bitter 'They're jealous of us–they need us and they hate us because they need us' writer thing. Which is probably true. I think that on the totem pole [of film production], writers are still pretty much the part of the pole that's stuck in the ground so that it will stay up."

Joss's success hasn't made him content, nor has it banished his view of himself as an outsider. He doesn't hesitate to take on his production company or his network when he feels poorly treated. Whedon was vocal in complaining about Fox's decision to position *Dark Angel* against *Angel* on Tuesday nights. "The fact that they put [*Dark Angel*] on opposite a show that they produce, thereby hurting it, shows that they really don't care," Whedon told *TV Guide Online.* "Their big picture is clearly *so* big that whatever I think and whatever I am doing doesn't matter, and I resent that.

writers are still pretty much the part of the pole that's stuck in the ground so that it will stay up. —Joss

But I am not a 'big-picture guy.' I'm just making my shows . . . I am not someone who can say, 'Work your schedule.'" Joss is also unhappy with *Dark Angel*'s name. "I watch [*Dark Angel*], and her name is not Angel, and she's not an angel, so why the [expletive] would they call it that?" he complains.

In the fall of 2002, Whedon tried a feat rarely seen in Hollywood, to produce three television series at the same time (*Buffy*, *Angel*, *Firefly*). Whedon promised to be deeply committed to each of these three series.

Before the season began he said, "This year I am going to be writing a bunch of original scripts in addition to everything else. I'm going to shoot four episodes total of all the three shows. I'm going

her name is not Angel, and she's not an angel, so why the [expletive] would they call it that? —Joss

to keep my hand in. Plus I'm doing stuff on the side just to relax, but don't tell anyone."

The "stuff on the side" was developing two other series (*Buffy the Animated Series* and *Ripper*), and writing movie scripts, comic books, and songs (he wrote a song for Anthony Head's solo album, *Music for Elevators*).

With all of these projects, and with his deep commitment to the quality of *Buffy* and *Angel*, why would he agree to launch *Firefly*, a high-profile project that would consume the bulk of his time? "Because I'm an idiot," Whedon joked at the time. But behind the jokes it's clear that Joss has an almost obsessive need to create new worlds. From a fan perspective, this may be a good thing, but did he take on too much? The 2002–2003 television season was one of his most challenging ever, as he tried to balance three programs (at least until the cancellation of *Firefly*). And with the departure of David Greenwalt, and Marti Noxon's maternity leave, Joss had to pick up much of the slack on *Buffy* and *Angel*.

Whedon wasn't willing to choose between his shows; he was committed to all of them and fervently denied that he detached himself from any of them. "I haven't been as hands-off as people like to think. This season, I was there, except when I was shooting the *Firefly* pilot. But yeah, everything I saw that I could have made better or had a different vision for, I go, 'Aaaarrgh!' But then, I've always done that."

So, was Joss headed for meltdown? At the beginning of the season his answer didn't inspire confidence. "I'm going to be more involved in *Angel* and *Buffy* even than I was last year. At the same time I'm going to be completely immersed in *Firefly*. And the trick to it all is increased efficiency. I'm also going to be home more, too. I have all of the New Year's resolutions. It really is a case of efficiency. We juggled some writers. They are all aware that they have to step up in ways they haven't before. That's [a] great opportunity for a writer or writer/producer. I have built this family, and although Daddy [Greenwalt] left and we all feel bad about that, I still have a huge extended family who are great, creative people. It's just a question of using the time and using the people and making sure that no one is ever not busy.

> I'm going to be more involved in *Angel* and *Buffy* even than I was last year. At the same time I'm going to be completely immersed in *Firefly*. And the trick to it all is increased efficiency. —Joss

"Is it impossible? Yes! Are we going to accomplish it? Yes! Because I won't abandon *Buffy* this late in the game. I won't abandon *Firefly* this early in the game and I especially won't abandon *Angel* right in the middle of its power. *Angel* is the one that no one really knows about. It's flying under the radar. It had such a good year."

Joss and a very preganant Kai Cole.

The cancellation of *Firefly* was difficult for Whedon, but it's clear that the show's problems had more to do with scheduling decisions and network impatience than with the show's quality, which was excellent. But where does he go from here?

The early seasons of *Buffy* allowed Joss to wrestle with the demons of his youth, with the alienation and misery of high school life. In the later seasons of *Buffy*, in *Angel*, and in *Firefly*, Joss is grappling with larger issues, with adulthood and responsibility in a dark and meaningless world.

But Whedon is entering a new world himself. He and his wife, Kai Cole, had a baby in December of 2002. Whedon promised himself that he would spend more time at home, a promise he found difficult to fulfill. But with a new child, Whedon will have to make some difficult choices.

If Whedon is like most fathers, his perspective on life and meaning will change profoundly with the birth of his child. Joss's work is intensely personal and connected with his history and worldview. It's fascinating to consider how a new child will affect his future work.

With all his accomplishments, it's sometimes difficult to remember that Joss is still a young man, that his best work is probably still ahead of him. And much of this work will likely be in film. Whedon has not abandoned this dream, but he is waiting to build the clout to do it his way. "I've gotten into this stage where basically I'm looking to develop something that I'm going to direct," Joss explains. "That's all about trying to make a movie that's made by me. Something that I can look at and say, 'That's good.' Everything that's happened before has sort of fed into this kind of attitude of 'Nobody cares about the writer.'

"The two worlds. Although people can move between them easily, they don't have much to do with each other. I'm still nobody. They're starting to notice me now, so that could change. But nobody in Hollywood seems to be saying, 'Hey, let's go talk to that "Sweden" guy.' When you get to, like, Stephen King level, then they want to film your sweatsocks. 'You wrote down a phone number? I'll option it!' But I'm not at that level."

But he's getting closer. It won't be long before Whedon gets an opportunity to write and direct a major iconic film, the next *Spider-Man* or *Batman*. Or he'll get the freedom to develop a world of his own, in the mode of *Star Wars*, *Terminator*, or *Alien*. Either way, expect Whedon to blossom into one of the great filmmakers of his generation. But don't expect him to go Hollywood. Joss will always be a writer first, a true fan, and a geek at heart.

Bibliography

Books

Lavery, David and Wilcox, Rhonda V. *Fighting the Forces: What's at Stake in Buffy the Vampire Slayer* (Rowman and Littlefield Publishers © 2002).

Articles

Brownfield, Paul. "Fangs Bared Over *Buffy*," Los *Angeles Times*, (April 23, 2001).

Goodykoontz, Bill. "A geeky pilgrimage to *Buffy* town," *The Arizona Republic* (July 18,2002).

Gross, Ed. "Joss the Vampire Scripter," *SFX* (Collector's Edition Vampire Special).

Huff, Richard. *The Daily News* (January 21, 2002).

McCollum, Charlie. "*Buffy* writer may be TV's best" *The Mercury News* (August 18, 2002).

Meltzer, Dana. "Raising the Stakes," *The Guardian* (London, January 5, 2002).

Mendoza, Manuel. "*Buffy* creator brings new meaning to prolific," *Dallas Morning News*,(Sept 8, 2002).

Neal, Justin. *Star Tribune* (September 25, 2001).

"Network outfoxed as *Buffy* delivers the cream," *Herald Sun*, (January 2, 2002).

Nussbaum, Emily. "Must-see Metaphysics," *New York Times*.

Rutenberg, Jim. *New York Times* (May 28, 2001).

Springer, Matt. "Singing Six's Praises," *Buffy Magazine* Issue No. 1 (February 5, 2002).

Udovitch, Mim. "What Makes Buffy Slay?" *Rolling Stone*, (May 11, 2000).

Websites

Amatangelo, Amy. "Interview with a Vampire Creator," *DishThis.com*
    www.dishthis.com/entertainment/wb/features/features_whedonint.html

Ash, Roger. "Joss Whedon Interview," *Westfield Comics*
    www.westfieldcomics.com/wow/low/low_int_051.html

Ausiello, Michael. "Emmy Body Slams *Buffy*," *TV Guide Online* (July 24, 2001).
    www.tvguide.com/newsgossip/insider/010724a.asp

_____. "WB Showdown: A Blow-by-Blow Account," *TV Guide Online* (August 15, 2001).
    www.tvguide.com/newsgossip/insider/010815c.asp

"*Buffy* Crosses the Pond" *Scifi.com*
  www.scifi.com/scifiwire/art-main.html?2002-06/11/13.00.tv
Ervin-Gore, Shawna. "Joss Whedon on *Fray*," *Dark Horse Online* (June 1, 2001).
  www.darkhorse.com/news/interviews/z_buffy/sku_00018int/index.html
Francis, Robert. "In Real Life," *BBC* (February 26 2002).
  www.bbc.co.uk/cult/buffy/reallife/jossinterview.shtml
Hirsch, Kimberly. "Biography," *Joss is a Hottie Online.*
  www.jossisahottie.com/bio.html
Jensen, Jeff. "Let 'Em Eat Stake," *Slayage.com*
  www.slayage.com/news/020609-joss_dvd.html
"Joss Whedon on Sex, Death, Gaping Holes and Horrible Things Ahead," *E!Online*
  www.eonline.com/Features/Features/Buffy/TheCreatorSpeaks/
Kuhn, Sarah. "Words of Whedon," *Chick Click* (July 4, 2001).
  entertainment.chickclick.com/articles/300877p1.html
Lee, Patrick. "Joss Whedon gets big, bad and grown up with *Angel*," *Science Fiction Weekly.*
  www.scifi.com/sfw/issue128/interview.html
Lilley, Ernest and Tellado, Tony. *Sci-Fi Talk*
  www.scifitalk.com/page5.htm
O'Hare, Kate. "*Angel's* Minear Discusses Producer Shake-Up," *ZAP2IT* (August 14, 2002).
  tv.zap2it.com/news/tvnewsdaily.html?27547
_____. "Sean Maher Lights Up Whedon's *Firefly*," *ZAP2IT* (June 25, 2002).
  tv.zap2it.com/news/tvnewsdaily.html?26626
_____. "Whedon Never Tires of Fresh Faces," *ZAP2IT* (August 7, 2002).
  tv.zap2it.com/news/tvnewsdaily.html?27427
Pierce, Scott D. "*Buffy* sings: Musical slayer is spectacular," *Desertnews.com*
  deseretnews.com/dn/view/0,1249,340007521,00.html?
Pond, Steve. "Sarah Michelle Gellar's New World Order" *Premiere.com* (October 2000).
  www.premiere.com/Premiere/Features/1000/buffy1.html
Robinson, Tasha. "Joss Whedon," *The Onion AV Club* (September 5, 2001).
  www.theonionavclub.com/avclub3731/avfeature_3731b.html
Schilling, Mary Kaye. "Vamping It Up," *Entertainment Weekly Online*
  www.ew.com/ew/report/0,6115,182495~3~0~behindscenesofbuffys,00.html
Wanda. "*Buffy* Creator Joss Whedon Talks Climaxes, Criticism and *Angel's* Fate" *E!Online.*
  www.eonline.com/Gossip/Wanda/Archive2002/020503d.html
Whedon, Joss. "Joss Whedon Speaks," *Fury.com.*
  fury.com/article/216.php
Whedon, Joss. "Joss Whedon speaks out about 'Once More With Feeling'" *Bronze Beta.*
  www.bronzebeta.com/Archive/Joss/Joss20011107.htm

Other

Bianculli, David. "Interview with Joss Whedon," *Fresh Air* on National Public Radio (November 8, 2002).
"Video Commentary," *Buffy the Vampire Slayer: Season 2* (DVD, June 11, 2002).

Index

Bye Bye Buffy!

As a special bonus, here's a transcript of
an interview Joss gave on 21 April, 2003.
If you haven't seen all of Buffy season seven, beware spoilers!

How are you planning to keep surprises for the finale, what with *Buffy*'s fan base and the Internet out there?

I can't. I gave up about a year ago trying to keep anything off of the Internet. Even if we had alternate endings, eventually you have to put together the one with the real ending, and somebody sees it before it goes out, on a satellite feed. The downside of the Internet is the destruction of surprise. However a lot of people don't go on it, or deliberately avoid spoilers. So they are the people I'm talking to the most. They are the people who want to see it pure, and understand that's the best way to see a story. The rest of them, I've given up on.

Is it tough being the leader, and do you feel anything that Buffy's been experiencing?

It is tough to be a leader. At one point they voted me out! [Laughs.] There is a difficulty in trying to be everywhere and be everything to everyone, and feeling a little cut off from everybody. That is definitely something I didn't know anything about until I became a leader of sorts, and I think that bled over [into the show] for sure.

How much is Xander still a part of you?

I have very bad vision in one eye. [Laughs because he's alluding to the episode in which Caleb poked out Xander's eye.] You know, a huge amount in fact. We pretty much made the statement when Dawn said, "Maybe that's your power. Seeing everything, knowing. Being the person who observes and reports." That's basically the same thing as being the writer, not the star. You couldn't have made him more of a proxy for me and the writers than that.

Over the series' run, how close has *Buffy* been to what you envisioned when you started?

It's been very close to what I envisioned, except that it grew up a lot more. When I started the show, I didn't know its full potential. I just sort of had the basic notion that 'it's tough to make it in high school'. [I thought that] it'll be funny, evolving, really scary, hip and something that people can relate to. I didn't know how good my actors would be, or how long we would go. How they would grow and change. And how far we could go with the medium, and what the networks would let us do. Did I know I would do a musical, or that Buffy would sleep with Angel and he would go bad? No, it just kept growing. The basic idea, that I think we are very true to in the last episode, is the empowerment of girls and the toughness of this life. That was always there, but it grew beyond my best intentions.

What's the status of some of the follow-up projects, including the animated series and Anthony Head's show?

Everything is pretty much in limbo right now. The animated series, there's nobody out there who has interest and enough money to make it look as good as it would have to. I don't want to make a cheesy version. The Giles thing is me kind of having to get my head wrapped around it. Now that I have a little free time, that's something I hope to do. There could be a spin-off at some time, but there's no talk of one, except for *Angel* [continuing], right now.

Once the show is gone, will it be hard to stop creating ideas for it? Is there kind of a 'phantom limb syndrome' soldier's experience?

Phantom story breaking. I think inevitably things will occur to me. Oh, they could do this, or they could go here. I'm constantly in the process of figuring out stories, and movies, and a lot of them aren't *Buffy*-related. I also have *Angel* and that's going to be 22 new stories we will have to break out in the same basic genre. I think I'll be able to put it to rest for a while.

Of the major characters who are with you now, which ones have developed in ways you never thought possible?

I really have to say all of them. When I started out, I knew my actors were good enough to do a light comedy-drama. I didn't know how powerful they would all be, and how deep we would be able to go with their characters. When we hired them, it was my first show and I didn't know what I was doing. I found out they were all much more than I expected.

Have you exceeded your expectations of yourself?

Yes, actually. I decided to create a TV show partially in film school. Nobody would hire me to direct, and I decided I would hire myself. In the process I'll sort of learn. I've been able to do that. But I've also learned more about writing in the last seven years than I did in the 30 before that.

In retrospect, is it possible there was a minor character in any episode that you wish you could have fleshed out, and done more with?

Generally speaking I can't think of one, because most of the time they end up sneaking back. Warren (Adam Busch) was a one-shot and so was Emma Caulfield. So when you see something that sparks, generally, if you can, you go back to it. Sunday, who I killed in the first episode of season four. She was played by Katherine Towne. She's somebody we all look back at and say we could have had a lot of fun with her, because she was something else. But I'm not big with regret.

If Sarah had wanted to come back and do another season, would you have had another season in you?

No. I knew this was my last season before Sarah made it official, although Sarah and I had talked about it a lot. I was pretty sure this was her last season too, but I had already sort of told the people close to me that even if Sarah had been offered a truckload of money to come back, or whatever it was that would change her mind, that I was done. That's not for lack of love or stories, just pure physical exhaustion. Just the grind of turning out the stories one by one. I was afraid I was about to slip, compromise, and just not care as much. Once you start doing that it shows. I knew it was the last year.

Is *Angel* coming back?

There's big love for it at the WB but I haven't heard anything. We have so much going for what's to come and they are in the loop on that. There's no reason for them not to pick it up, but I've been wrong before. I'd be very surprised if we didn't come back. We are entering in a whole new arena and a whole new way of telling these stories next season. So, there's a huge amount of life left.

It's been a strange season on *Angel*, because everything took place in approximately two weeks [from the characters' point of view]. But the intensity never let up, and I really do feel like we pulled it off. Next season, we hope to keep that extraordinary over-the-top melodrama and action that sort of defines *Angel*, in a way that *Buffy* wasn't. But we are also going to take it to a new place. A way to generate stories that is not so totally internal, so that it will not be one giant two-week adventure. That lets people who have never seen it sort of get into it a little more.

Has the door been left open for more *Buffy*?

Yes, we did not destroy the entire fabric of the universe in the last episode. Some people even lived. There's definitely a door open for more series or a movie. You name it.

Will any of the *Buffy* principles move to *Angel*?

I think we can count on a few of them visiting. I can't say for sure if anyone will move there. *Angel* has a strong ensemble and I definitely want to see some of my *Buffy* guys go in there. It's great to mix up the energy. We don't have any official plans about any of them becoming full-time. We are partially waiting for the pick up to finalize.

Did you always know you were going to develop Buffy through the years, or did she kind of reveal herself gradually?

What I knew was that I wasn't going to pretend they were in high school the whole time. I didn't want them to be 35 and sophomores. That's just sad. The one thing I'm committed to, and the one thing that really jazzes me in TV, is change. The shows that really affected me, besides the *Masterpiece Theater* stuff, was like *Hill Street Blues*, which was all about people you know, doing things you didn't expect them to do. It wasn't about the same warm fuzzy, or action. TV is so much about sameness and the comfort of knowing what you are going to get. *Hill Street Blues* was a show that didn't do that.

So, I knew that I wanted her to develop. Exactly who she would develop into, I really had no idea. Somewhere along the way, the way she developed had to do with Sarah, and what she brought to the character. Some of it had to do with the different themes we wanted to explore. Some of it we just fell into. I didn't want to be static, but I had no idea who she would be.

The First came in 1998 with 'Amends'. Did you know you were going to bring it back for the ending of it all?

No, I didn't. I used The First as a device solely to tell the story about Buffy and Angel that I wanted to tell. But then that's what happens with the show. You are looking for something and suddenly you realize it is sitting in your lap. That everything you need is right there. It seemed the perfect villain for the finale, because it's what they all fear and what they have all been through, personified. It seemed serendipitous.

Can you talk more about the new direction for *Angel*?

I can't be too specific about it. Basically it means that they aren't going to be sitting around the pouffe in the hotel waiting for the phone to ring, fighting with each other. We are going to see them working on a much broader scale. A lot of different milieus and a lot of new venues for them. This year, of which I'm enormously proud, was a very internal drama. While I want to keep all of that character stuff and integrity and intensity, I want to open them up to a much broader, stranger life in L.A. And that's what's going to happen.

What lessons did you learn from series finales from the past?

There's been a bunch that I've seen. Most of the lessons I've learned from other shows were cautionary tales. It's very hard to pay off something that is going to cover everybody. In a way I felt like I had already done that - in season five. When we didn't know if we were going to come back. Part of it was self-indulgent. I loved the end of *M*A*S*H*. I watched and cried as much as anyone else. At the end of the day though, [do we need] 70 minutes for the last *Family Ties*? It's very easy to think so much of what you are doing that you forget what you really need to do is turn out an episode that is really great. I knew the message I wanted to give, and the story I wanted to tell in the last episode for a long time. So, I felt like I had that strength. Of course, you are paralyzed with terror because you worry that people will say, "This one doesn't measure up." Or they'll say you didn't go out on a great one. You want it to be great. [But] if you spend your time thinking, this line has to be great, you never write anything! So in a way, you have to think of it as just another episode.

The other cautionary tale I would cite is *Miami Vice*. Where the ad campaign said, "They saved the best for last!" So I watched it, and it was just another lame ass episode. And I was like, "Oh, they lied!" I tried to save enough for the last episode so that people would say they went out with a bang, but they didn't go out banging a drum. They went out making their show.

In terms of the theme [of the *Buffy* finale], can you share that without giving out the specifics?

You know that we've dealt with all of the potential slayers and Buffy's attempt to lead, [and] Willow dealing with her fear. Everyone is dealing with their insecurities and their place. The season has really been about power. At least that's what we started talking about, the mission statement of the show was: This girl has power. Nobody knows, nobody sees it, they don't respect her, they don't get it, but she has enormous power. This episode is about that. It deals very specifically with how she decides to use that power, and what she thinks of it. That to me is very important.

Will it end with her in a better mood than she's been in lately?

Assuming she lives. You never know. I love killin' folk.

Whom is a finale for? Is it for the viewer, the writer, or the cast and crew?

It's for the viewer. I honor this cast and crew enormously, but at the end of the day the finale has to be for the viewer. There will be a little shout out to things, usually they are old episodes or things that long-time viewers will understand. It's not about anyone but the viewers. It comes from the writer and it has to reflect what they believe and want. But the fact of the matter is, I write as a fan. I write as a someone who wants to know what's going to happen next on *Buffy*, not just, "Oh, what do I feel like talking about today?"

At what point did you say to yourself, "This is how I want it to end"?

I've known for over a year. I've known since last year exactly what I wanted to do for the last episode... I take that back. It was some time over the summer that I came back and pitched the ending to the writers. They went, "Oh, that makes sense." We sort of had the basic structure for the season laid out before we even started. It's all been headed for one particular place, which you know sometimes makes things easier, sometimes harder. In our case I think it's helped a lot.

There's been a lot of academic deconstruction of the show. Has any of that informed what you are doing in any way?

I haven't actually read much of the academic deconstruction, although I'm glad that there is some. What's written about the show seldom affects us. It does sometimes, when someone points out an aspect of something we didn't realize was there. Sometimes there will be a criticism that we'll take to heart. By and large we are in our little sweatbox of the arts, just kind of riffing. We talk a lot about what everything means, so for there to be an academic study of the show on many different levels makes perfect sense to us, because we think about all of those levels. Well, sometimes people come up with stuff that we really can't comprehend. But we don't use [the academic deconstruction] as our basis. Our basis is the everyday. You are growing up in this position, what does it feel like?

Do you think in terms of novelistic themes?

I don't approach [stories] in the way that I believe *Babylon 5* had a whole [pre-planned] five-year arc when it started. This isn't that kind of story. It has the randomness of common life, because that is what we set out to portray. Everyday troubles sort of blown up into grand stories. You can't really predict what is going to happen. You can go about a year in advance, tops. You have to know everything you need to know to keep going, but if you know more than that, you can trap yourself. Then you realize this character doesn't have chemistry with that one, or this character really pops in a different way than we expected - and we should pursue that. But you are stuck with the other thing because you are wed to it. So, I like to keep things kind of open.

There was an article in the press about the current world situation, and the impending clash on *Buffy*. Do you think that's true?

Actually, we found ourselves in a terrible situation. I do not support our President's actions in pretty much anything he does. The last thing in the world I ever wanted was for any of Buffy's rhetoric to be compared to anything he was saying. Yet he goes to war and ostensibly we have basically a war on *Buffy*. It was very much a concern of the writers and myself to try and stress the pain and uncertainty and the emotion of it, rather than the gung ho 'let's go get 'em' of war. Because none of us advocate the idea of war. I certainly didn't support this particular action to go in [to Iraq]. We found ourselves hoping the emotion would come through and people wouldn't misuse our rhetoric for the purpose of saying, "See? Buffy likes war."

You mentioned *Hill Street Blues, Family Ties, M*A*S*H, Miami Vice*. There are a lot of people who would put *Buffy* in the same category of popularity as those shows, yet far fewer people watched *Buffy* compared to them. Can you talk about that?

Buffy was designed to become a pop culture icon, and she became that. So she exists beyond her ratings. (Laughs.) It's true we've never found an enormous audience. We've never been on one of the giant networks. At the same time we have retained our cult status, in that our viewership has never been as large as the awareness of us. But *Buffy* is not designed to exclude anybody, because I don't believe in that. I didn't want to make a teen show that said, "Look how stupid grownups are." I wanted to make a teen show that said, "Look how hard it is to do this. To live through this. And, by the way, when you get to be a grownup it doesn't get easier. At the same time, *Buffy the Vampire Slayer* isn't a show some people are going to switch on. That's just the way it is, and that doesn't bother me.

Do you think its cachet will continue to grow over the years, like some of the other shows you mentioned?

Well, it has the opportunity that some of the other shows didn't because it is out on DVD, and it's out now before it looks wicked dated. Although some of the outfits from season one are pretty funny! The thing we were trying to do was tell epic, timeless stories on a small, emotional scale. That sort of thing, when it is done right, certainly can live on. Will it? I don't know. I do know the character as a concept has affected the way people think about heroines, heroes [and] what boys will watch - and that's more important a legacy than if they are still watching the episodes.

As you got to the end, was it in any way freeing? The episode with Xander getting his eye poked out was pretty violent...

We didn't go, "Hey let's do violence, because we can!" We wanted to let people know the stakes were high. We are definitely not doing stuff because we can get a way with it. I've never been interested in extremes of gore and whatnot. But I will say that a couple of times when we were talking about things in the finale we would say, "Well, what are they going to do? Cancel us?"

Can you talk about how our friends from *Firefly* ended up being two really bad people on *Buffy* and *Angel*?

They are just terrible people. (Laughs.) It was very simply a case where we had created the characters. It didn't come from me. I was worried it would be too incestuous. It was Marti [Noxon] in one case and Tim [Minear] in another. They were like, "Hey, we have the people; we know their names and their phone numbers." Both Nathan and Gina are bigger than life, and we knew they would bring up the story telling and give it an epic quality. They would give us some performances we could count on, and which are very different from what they did on *Firefly*. I thought, "Who cares if it's incestuous, most people didn't watch *Firefly* anyway..." Hell, I did. If you have an actor you know can get the job done, and you haven't seen them do it 400 times... Nathan had never played a villain, and when Gina was playing Zoe she didn't get to be all-pretty and smile all of the time. It was stuff we knew they had in them, that they hadn't shown us on screen. So it was a good opportunity for them, and I'm not stupid. If I've got the guys and I know they can do it... Besides, they are wonderful people who make the set a better place to be around.

Are you in talks with any of the networks to do some kind of spin-off?

Right now, I'm in talks with sleepin.' What I basically told people is that we thought about it, the opportunity kind of passed us by, and everybody is kind of beat up. It's been seven years. We all need to take a break, give it a few months and let our brains heal. Then I think we'll start to see if there's somebody we are so attached to we can build off...

Visit:

Take a tour
through Joss Whedon's brain

Test yourself at the Joss Whedon quiz

Win a *Buffy the Vampire Slayer*
Season 4 DVD

And more...

BUFFY MAGAZINE!

FREE VALENTINE'S CARD!

FREE POSTER! NEW EPISODES REVIEWED!

Buffy
the vampire slayer

CHASING AMY
Elizabeth Anne Allen on her return to *Buffy*

DECONSTRUCTING ANYA

Issue 48
Mar 2003
£2.85
(Cover 1 of 2)

Exclusive set report on origin episode!

SUNNYDALE NEWS
The latest on *Buffy Season Seven*, plus *Angel Season Four*

I'm the Slayer

∏ SALE AT ALL GOOD ∏EWSAGE∏TS!

CALL 01536 764 646 ∓O SUBSCRIBE

GRAPHIC NOVEL STAKE OUT!

ALL NEW, BUFFY ADVENTURES FROM TITAN BOOKS

Available from all good bookshops, or telephone Titan Mail Order on 01536 76 46 46.
(Office hours open Monday – Friday 9am-5pm.)

We love to hear from our readers. Why not email us at:
r e a d e r . f e e d b a c k @ t i t a n e m a i l . c o m